QUIT DRINKING

UNDERSTANDING ALCOHOLISM, REMOVING THE
ADDICTION FROM YOUR LIFE AND BELIEVING IN
YOUR FUTURE SOBER SELF.

REBECCA DOLTON

CONTENTS

QUIT DRINKING

UNDERSTANDING ALCOHOLISM, REMOVING THE ADDICTION FROM YOUR LIFE AND BELIEVING IN YOUR FUTURE SOBER SELF.

Rebecca Dolton

INTRODUCTION

My goal is not to just help you quit drinking. I know that the title may have been a little misleading. What I really want is to also help you wake up and find your way again. The modern life- style and, in our particular case, drinking have placed a lot of us into a deep slumber.

Through awareness, acceptance, and the commitment to create the positive changes in your life that you so passionately desire, your drinking problems will naturally disappear. If you're reading this book, it means that the silence between commercials, those seconds of thought at a stoplight, and those moments of sobriety have all allowed your inner voice to reach you and convince you to get back on your path once more.

With the increased velocity in which information is being exchanged in our current era, a lot of people feel lost in the sea of possibilities. Many of us look to drinking as an escape route, a means to avoid this tragic and painful experience we call life. Reality can feel really boring, even meaningless at times.

You may be looking to escape from depression, anxiety, shame, boredom, or anger. I want to teach you how to use depression, anxiety, shame, boredom, and anger to your advantage.

We live in an age of comfort and easily accessible information where we don't have to hunt for our food anymore. You only need to lift a couple of fingers in order to get food and entertainment, so you would think people would be happy, right? Shouldn't we feel less lonely since we're all connected through the internet? What could be the reason that suicide, depression, anxiety, and addiction are at an all-time high?

What kinds of connections could exist between our modern lifestyle and addiction? Our avoidance of pain through sedation has made us lose touch with ourselves which is why people have become so unaware of their own emotions, actions, and motivations. Have you ever met somebody who wasn't aware of themselves? Whose right hand didn't know what the left hand was doing?

I mean isn't that the reason why many of us drink? So that we don't have to be present anymore or so we can ignore the expectations people have of us? Some people call it 'just having fun,' but when we over do it, there is often an underlying issue which can explain our loss of control. It's quite difficult to deal with somebody who isn't self-aware, somebody who thinks they're always right.

When we're not present or when we let our unconscious mind take over and we flick the autopilot switch 'on.' The next day we find ourselves dealing with feelings of shame and embarrassment since we may have done things we wouldn't normally do if we had been completely conscious. We try to shrug it off and just say it was because we were drunk while deep inside feelings of guilt linger.

When I say I am going to help you 'wake up,' I don't mean this in a philosophical or mystical way. I'll be providing practical steps on how to snap out of an automatic way of life. Waking up is the first step to recovery from addiction. Afterward, I will be helping you challenge the way you see yourself and the world around you.

In other words, I want to help you deprogram yourself. Society and biology have both wired your brain for addiction.

By the end of this work, I would like you to be able to answer the following question: **Why do you want to recover?**

The answer to this question is key to your recovery; keep that in mind as we progress through our work.

My Story

I had an extremely destructive experience with alcohol which is what inspired me to help others through their struggle. My partner was an alcoholic, and the worst part was that he didn't know it. I had never been so close to somebody going through the process of becoming addicted to alcohol, so I didn't realize it was becoming an issue until it was already out of control.

Looking back, the behavioral patterns and his state of denial were classic descriptions of becoming addicted. He would drink when he was happy, but he would also drink when he was sad, stressed, or in any kind of pain. It had become his 'go-to' coping mechanism.

Rarely would we spend time together where drinking wasn't involved. It was as if it was his only source of joy in life. When I tried suggesting that maybe he should cut down on his drinking, he would feel attacked and say I was trying to control him.

The situation started to get out of hand when he would lose control and become aggressive. One time, he kicked a hole in our wall while screaming insults and blaming me for his misfortunes. I never felt in physical danger, but the constant blame eventually hurt my self-esteem. If somebody repeatedly tells you, "You're the problem," you start believing it. I started feeling like there was something inherently bad about myself. The instability and emotional abuse really took its toll on me.

Through the whole relationship, I would try to be supportive and talk things over with him. It was exhausting. He would never recognize that he was contributing a lot of the problems. He would always justify his aggressive and abusive behaviors saying that is my fault for one reason or the other. It was nearly impossible to get an apology from him.

To make matters worse, his mother was extremely enabling. She would support his views and continuously justify his behavior. She made excuses for his behavior, no matter how abhorrent, by saying that he acted the way he did because life had been 'unfair' to him.

This enablement allowed him to continue to shift any responsibility for his actions to anything but himself. He projected his flaws on others and blamed society or his upbringing for the state of his life. This enabling process had been happening for years before I got there. It seemed like his mother couldn't bear the fact that there may have been something wrong with her son because that could consequently mean that her parenting was faulty as well.

It got to the point that I had to distance myself emotionally and physically. This felt terrible because I felt like I was leaving him when he needed me most when he really needed my support. All my friends told me to leave. Everyone I knew said I was crazy for staying as long as I had. I guess when you love someone you can't just get up and run away at the first sign of trouble but, when you are in the bubble, it's hard to know what to do and when.

I decided that by staying I was enabling the behavior to continue, and I was getting very depressed myself. It was the worst feeling in the world having to leave the person that you love most. It was so clear to me then what was happening and that I was powerless to make any sort of difference. They would only change if they wanted to only when they recognized that they had a problem. They were in a bubble of denial that was reinforced by influential people in their world and I was the outsider causing trouble.

I promised myself that I would never allow myself to be in what was an abusive relationship again. It doesn't matter why or how a partner is abusive, it's very important to maintain your own mental health. That said, it's very hard to see someone so clearly damaged and traumatized from events in their past and not want to help and support them, especially when you know they have a wonderful side to them.

Looking back at this time, that was what confused me the most. How could this talented, smart, funny, and beautiful man become such a monster when he had a drink? The change was sometimes a total reversal from the person that I fell in love with.

I know my story isn't unique and I know there are people who have suffered much more than I have. I wanted to explain why I was motivated to write this book. I have spent a lot of time with people who have a problem with alcohol, they're not bad people, you're not a bad person, they can change and so can you. I wanted to do something for you to make the process of recovery much easier for you. The first step was to pick up this book which I'm very glad you have done. You have reached out for help and I'm honored that you have allowed me to speak to you through these pages.

This is exactly what I want to help you remember: I want to help you remember how wonderful you are and that you have been led astray from your path by internal and external forces. Internally, your fears, doubts, and regrets have distorted the way you see yourself and your relationship with others. Externally, society has planted the seeds of envy and greed through consumerism.

The road ahead is not easy but you have already taken the biggest step, well done! The rest we can do together.

About the Method

Some of the knowledge in this book comes from ancient literature and teachings based on alchemy, Eastern mysticism, and Christianity. All this knowledge, however, has now been put to the test through the lens of science. The methods described in this work are largely based on Acceptance and Commitment Therapy (ACT) and Meaning-Centered Therapy (MCT) or Logotherapy.

ACT is a great acronym since it really describes the practical action-oriented approach of this method. The focus is going to be on meaningful ACTion.

Have you ever experienced a feeling of emptiness, like something is missing?

To be clear this work has no particular spiritual or religious inclination. It's made for any human to be able to adapt our techniques and put them to use, regardless of their beliefs.

I promise you won't look at your life's history or your future the same way after we're done here.

The practical essence of this work does require you to do the exercises. Reading the book alone won't yield any result; this is a call to action. Rewiring your brain takes work, discipline, motivation, and forgiveness.

The process you're about to undergo will help you change your relationship to drinking as naturally as possible.

1

WHAT ARE WE UP AGAINST?

Alcohol Abuse and Society

You're hungover, thinking about the questionable things you did or said the night before, hesitant to check the messages on your phone. You're filled with feelings of regret and embarrassment because no matter how hard you try, you seem to keep making the same mistakes. You're wondering if you will ever change, if you will ever be able to prioritize your ambitions and your responsibilities over your drinking and social habits. The next time you feel that you are not in control, please remember there are 66.7 million other people going through the same types of struggles you are (HHS, 2016). That's how many people reported they struggled with alcohol abuse in a study carried out in the United States. Studies like this one have been carried out across the world yielding similar results. You are not alone, alcohol abuse is a real issue, and it can't go unchecked. Some can overcome it, while others often fail to recover.

So what is the difference between those who recover and those who don't?

We may say to ourselves, "It's just a phase, I've got it under control," or, "I'll be more careful next time," and that may be true for a while. With the passing of time and before you know it, you will create an emotional dependency to alcohol if you haven't already. As with the creation of any habit, it takes time and repetition. The fact that it is an enjoyable activity makes the creation of the habit that much easier. You may not be able to enjoy yourself in a social setting the same way without alcohol, for instance. Alternatively, you may not be able to cope with the frustrations of life without a stress reliever at the end of the week or even at the end of the day. We all have our reasons for having a drink and we rarely feel like it's an issue.

In recent years, the use of alcohol but, more importantly, the abuse of alcohol has become a problem with worldwide repercussions.The magnitude of these repercussions has incited the World Health Organization to create a global strategy to help mitigate the damages caused by alcohol abuse (HHS, 2016). When we think of alcohol abuse, we might think of hormonal teenagers who don't have any self-restraint. The fact that the WHO is getting involved means that there may be more to it than that. Alcohol is considered to be one of the higher ranking causal factors for disability, disease, and fatality in any given nation.

There are more subtle aspects of alcohol consumption that cause great harm, though. Popularly known but often ignored, alcohol damages our gut and liver. Socially relevant collateral such as child abuse and neglect may be less obvious to all, except to those who have lived in this type of environment. We have all heard the stories of drunken family members who torment their loved ones while taking no responsibility for their actions. Even if physical abuse isn't present, neglect is an equally damaging experience for a child. Unfortunately, those who experience these types of abuse as children often repeat the same cycle of fear and hate, reproducing the damage once caused to them (Samuels, 2001).

Alcohol has a strong relationship with violence, mainly due to the fact that when we consume it, we impair the parts of our brain involved in self-control and risk analysis. Along with our loss of self-control, emotional regulation decreases as well. Primal feelings of anger, fright, or sadness, in turn, take control of us.

This loss of control may provide a clue to understand why alcohol is involved in 3.3 million deaths every year, accounting for 5.9 percent of deaths worldwide (Hendershot et. al. as cited in HHS, 2016). This fact would lead you to the belief that alcohol use would be taboo or at least frowned upon much like tobacco use is nowadays. It is quite the opposite, though: alcohol is the single most socially accepted drug. It is considered classy, edgy, or cool in certain cultures. This perception of alcohol has allowed different countries and different states to maintain a posture of low priority against the substance.

What is it externally about alcohol that draws you in?

Media and marketing agencies are largely responsible for portraying alcohol as a fun and friendly substance to all age groups. From celebrities such as Marilyn Manson and Bob Dylan promoting their own brands of alcohol to college sports events being sponsored by beer breweries, these industries are only out to make a buck. They don't really care for our wellbeing, and that is something that we must keep in mind. Sure, they want us to have fun and like their product, but that is only because they want us to buy more of it. By no means do they actually care about our happiness or our fulfillment, we simply cannot entrust our happiness to those who are only out to profit.

Alcohol Use Disorder (AUD) and Individuals

How do we know we have an issue?

We are all familiar with alcohol's charming qualities. We go out for a night intending to only have a drink or two at most, and then find ourselves ordering our ninth or tenth drink. We may say things like, "Oh, I've earned it. I deserve to have a little fun," to justify our temporary loss of control. In fact, the loss of control can be the main goal for some, exemplified by the phrase, "Loosen up! Have a drink!" This phrase references the part of drinking alcohol that allows you to forget about your worries through the reduction of anxiety. You should not feel guilty for not being able to control yourself when it comes to having a drink. It is in the very nature of alcohol to make you want to take more risks and it directly impairs that part of you in charge of self restraint. We are talking about a pleasurable experience that raises our confidence, therefore it is understandable that many of us enjoy the feeling we have when we become drunk.

You can have one pint or ten beers or six shots of tequila: the issue isn't how much alcohol you drink, the issue lies in your relationship to drinking.

Mental health professionals in America use the term Alcohol Use Disorder (AUD) to refer to alcoholism. The term includes both the type of people who drink every-day, and those who drink excessive amounts once in a while, commonly referred to as binge drinking. You don't have to be drinking everyday to put yourself and others at risk. It only takes a single step in the wrong direction to turn an enjoyable night into a catastrophic accident.

The phrase, "Drinking more or for a longer period than intended," (American Psychiatric Association, 2013, p.490) from the Diagnostic and Statistical Manual Of Mental Disorders (DSM) is one of the determining factors that allow us to know if we have a problem. The keyword in that sentence is 'intended.' The DSM (2013) points out three additional factors present in AUD: craving, tolerance and withdrawal. Craving refers to intense desires we may feel to consume alcohol.

For some people the craving to drink may be triggered when they find themselves in a social situation, perhaps at a party. The discomfort felt by people with high levels of social anxiety is dealt with by many through the use of alcohol. A sort of crutch is adopted, and all those internal worries about how others view you or how you see yourself seem to fade away as you drink. Your new-found liquid confidence provides you the strength to mingle and speak with strangers. In these scenarios, alcohol is used to replace the process an individual has to go through to learn the social skills necessary to interact with others. The need to drink in these scenarios is one manifestation of craving, referred to as social drinking. Cravings for social drinkers are triggered by a need to avoid discomfort or pain in social settings.

We will come to see that pain exists in life for a reason, and it is not to be numbed but instead listened to.

Cravings have another harmful characteristic to them, a priority shifting effect. This happens when the desires to consume alcohol become so prevalent that they start to outweigh our other priorities. Drinking is prioritized over our ambitions and responsibilities. Often we negotiate with ourselves and look to convince ourselves that we do have enough time to drink tonight, when in fact, we may have school, work, or other domestic tasks to carry out in the morning. We would rather drink in these scenarios, compromising our academic and professional responsibilities. Drinking can become more important than looking after your children affectionately and attentively. This shift in priorities is a common factor of addictions in general, not specific to alcohol dependency. These are all signs of problematic cravings culminating in intense moments where you put your desire for a drink in front of your physical and social integrity, when the things once most dear to you are considered secondary.

Tolerance is the second factor that is intrinsically tied to craving. Through repeated satiation of our desire to have a drink, we will come to notice that we begin to require more alcohol to feel that same effect we used to with less.

In many cultures, the acquisition of tolerance is celebrated as an achievement. Phrases like, "You can really hold your drink!" exemplify this idea. Drinking games and competitions are commonplace in college. Though seemingly harmless, these activities accustom us to drink to our very limits and often beyond them. We become less sensitive to the bodily cues that tell us we are reaching a limit.

We all understand very well what happens when the limit is surpassed. Our body will either attempt to recover itself from intoxication by vomiting and/or we will enter a state of near unconsciousness where we are mentally and physically impaired, while having little to no regard for our safety. Unfortunately, tolerance causes us to consume more alcohol, consequently increasing our dependence on the substance.

Finally, withdrawal is inevitably connected to the first two factors of AUD. Hangovers and the associated problems that are caused by chronic and acute use of alcohol are what we are referring to here. Often you will drink again the morning after, or throughout the afternoon to try to chase away the uncomfortable withdrawal symptoms we experience. Symptoms such as lethargic and depressive states of mind, indigestion, and sleep problems. This last symptom is much subtler and is linked to a more chronic version of alcohol dependency.

While sleep disorders are associated with the more chronic effects of withdrawal, hangovers on the other hand can be associated with the acute consumption of alcohol. We will be exploring in great detail the mechanisms by which we experience psychological and physical withdrawal symptoms in later chapters.

Diagnostics and categories are made to help us understand what other people are going through. By no means should we feel labeled since it doesn't have to be a permanent state of being, and these labels definitely should not define us as a person. I say this so you don't just automatically place yourself in the label of 'addict' or 'alcoholic.'

You must understand that you are not alone, that many of us have been through the struggle. At the same time, you have to be able to forgive yourself, to let go of any feelings of guilt. A lack of self-love can be a motivating factor for many people who abuse alcohol. That is why it is so important to stop beating yourself up and understand that recovering from alcohol dependency is not an easy task.

By reading these lines right now, you have come a long way. You have already taken your first step towards awareness. Awareness may be the first step, but awareness without insight can lead to frustration.

Often we come to understand that we have an issue, but find ourselves without the tools to resolve it. That is what I am here to help you with. In the following chapter, I would like to assist you in the process of weighing the benefits and costs that come with drinking so that you can make an educated decision on what path to choose.

2

WHY STOP? WHY DON'T WE STOP?

L ike I said, awareness without insight will lead to frustration. I am sure you have made attempts to change your ways and know just how frustrating it is to fight against yourself constantly. You are not just fighting against yourself, though. There are other factors that cause you to consume excessive amounts of alcohol and in destructive ways. We shall look at some of the factors that cause alcohol addiction.

Who is in Control?

Typically, when you ask somebody to picture an addict in their mind, the first images that will come up are of a homeless person or somebody involved in criminal activities. Addiction has been severely stigmatized. This is why the concept of a functioning addict remains obscure. The truth of the matter is that you don't have to be socially dysfunctional in order to be addicted to a behavior or a substance.

When it comes to cravings and not being able to control your drinking habits, I really want to ask you to not to beat yourself up over it. There are so many factors at play that work against you. It's understandable for you to struggle to gain control when you may have your genetics predisposing you to addiction, and the alcohol industries are targeting you as a consumer at the same time. Alcohol is designed to act upon the reward centers of your brain and, to make matters worse, there are even microorganisms within your gut that crave the substance (Ende et, al., 2019). It really brings up the question: are we truly the ones making the decisions when it comes to drinking?

It is common among ex-alcoholics in Alcoholic Anonymous (AA) support groups to tell stories about how their parents were addicted to alcohol themselves. This should not come as a surprise because there is a vast amount of research indicating that having a genetic predisposition to alcohol increases the likelihood of us becoming addicted to alcohol by over 50% (Saraswat, 2016). A predisposition only matters if you drink, but if you do drink, then your genes are definitely not going to be on your side. Let's keep in mind that genetics can predispose us but they can't determine us. We can take responsibility for our actions, but we can also be understanding with ourselves if we relapse.

Do you have parents, or grandparents that suffered from alcohol dependencies?

The alcohol industry is another entity that encourages us to consume alcohol. These industries have funded large amounts of research so that they can come up with the most efficient ways to sell their product. One of the more taboo fields of research is the field of planting subconscious suggestions, or as it is more popularly known, subliminal messaging. These topics are no longer as mysterious and controversial as they used to be. Our brain can process messages emotionally, before we even become conscious of the information we are processing (Mahoney et. al., 2014). Meaning that even if we don't read a Facebook post, or a message on a billboard, it will still have an impact on the way we evaluate the products emotionally. This is a well known fact and a strategy implemented in alcohol-related propaganda. They implicitly sell us ideas like *alcohol will make you cooler*, or *it can make you popular with the ladies*, etc. These ideas are planted in our brains without us even being aware of it.

Once the propaganda gets to you or your friends and you do start drinking, alcohol has a peculiar effect on your brain. It affects neurotransmitters in your brain such as dopamine which is associated with our pleasure and pain receptors. Dopamine is largely related to pain relief. So when you drink alcohol you are sending pleasure and pain relief signals to your brain which not only numbs pain but also makes your body want more of the substance.

Dopamine has always been nature's way of telling us we are on the right path.

Animals and humans alike know how to seek pleasure and avoid pain due to their dopamine receptors. When you find something that causes you joy and satisfaction occurs, you release dopamine in your brain.

Usually dopamine is released in small amounts during these pleasurable moments of your life, moments such as looking at your children smile, petting a dog, or being intimate with your partner. Drinking provides these chemicals in much higher concentrations which is one of the reasons we enjoy it so much, and why we want to continue drinking. The fact that these endorphins are released in such high doses when we drink makes other pleasurable activities in life seem less important.

The release of dopamine during alcohol consumption ties in to the deprioritizing effect of alcohol. Our brain starts to perceive drinking as a lot more pleasurable than any other activity that used to cause us joy. Dopamine is very closely related to our attentional processes which makes us focus even more on the substance that caused the dopamine release.

When our brain becomes accustomed to the large amounts of pleasure that drinking brings, it dilutes other types of pleasures life provides us, pleasures that are earned through hard work and dedication, for example. It's much easier to pick up a bottle of whiskey and feel good than it is to cultivate one of your talents.

Immediate gratification is a trap that many of us fall into. Although drinking brings pleasure, it isn't long-lasting pleasure and it is a pleasure that leaves an existential emptiness which we try to fill by drinking some more. Long-lasting pleasures are those we receive through fulfillment and achievements.

The enteric nervous system is the channel by which microorganisms influence us to consume alcohol. This nervous system is located in our gut, and it is the reason a lot of people are starting to call our gut *the second brain*. Our gut is home to trillions of microorganisms, from fungi to many kinds of bacteria. These bacteria can actually influence the way we perceive taste and the food preferences we have (Singh et. al., 2017). They do this by communicating with our brain through the vagus nerve.

There is a strain of fungi called Candida Albicans. This strain in particular thrives on high amounts of simple sugars found in our intestinal tract and guess what else? Ethanol, the compound alcohol is made of, is one of those sugars it loves. It has been shown that this micro-organism can stimulate cravings for alcohol. Candida Albicans is a pathogenic fungi and is only looking out for its own well-being. It creates roots in your small intestine causing holes in it. The more we feed it, the more its population increases, consequently increasing the cravings for alcohol we may feel (Ende et, al., 2019).

There are many entities who are looking out for their own interest at the cost of our well-being. We really have to ask ourselves if we want to be controlled by these parasitic microorganisms or equally the alcohol industry.

Drinking as a Coping Mechanism

There are some painful activities in life that people pursue intentionally. People who love spicy foods and those who thoroughly enjoy exercise can relate to this idea. When you eat a freshly picked habanero or ghost pepper and take a bite out of it, it causes a great deal of pain. Yet to many, it is a quite enjoyable activity, some would even go as far as to describe it as an uplifting and stress relieving experience similar to that of drinking coffee. This seems much more intense than drinking coffee, though. This is the same way some people describe going for a long run as being a very relaxing activity while being exhilarating at the same time.

When you are eating that pepper or lifting those weights, the pain that you cause your body triggers a release of dopamine. This release of dopamine is meant to relieve pain, stress, and anxiety which is why these seemingly painful activities can turn very pleasurable. Dopamine is how our body helps us deal with physical and emotional pain.

Through repetitive overstimulation of our dopaminergic system by drinking, we can eventually cause an imbalance or reduction of the presence of dopamine. Dopamine is a finite neurotransmitter produced in our brain and our gut. Low levels of dopamine are correlated with depressive disorders. This means that by consuming alcohol in excessive amounts we are bound to make our life dull and to be more sensitive to both physical and emotional pain.

Once we've created an imbalance in our dopaminergic system, the moments when we are supposed to feel pleasure from an enjoyable activity, we will feel a lot less of it than we should. We won't get as happy when we meet our long lost friend again, or when we look at a beautiful sunset. The small joys of life cannot provide the dopamine levels that our brain is accustomed to receiving from drinking.

It's quite ironic. A lot of people look at drinking as a way to escape the boredom of their sober life, only to end up feeling even less joy from life's pleasures.

This state of perceiving our life as boring and grey is called anhedonia. Anhedonia is an inability to experience pleasure. If we are not able to gain pleasure from the small wins that everyday life provides us, we start to lose motivation. Things start to seem pointless and life becomes quite painful. If you don't have a reason to get up and go to work everyday, it can become a very daunting task.

Something like having a successful work week seems small and meaningless to us when we have become emotionally dependent on alcohol. Without a real cause to be happy, it is understandable how you would turn to drinking to rid yourself from all the perceived meaningless pain and suffering that life has to offer. The problem here is that if everything else becomes superfluous, we start to plan our life around the one thing that brings us joy, that brings us relief from pointless suffering. We start to plan our life around drinking.

We begin to spend more time carrying out activities that bring us closer to the substance. The friends we hang out with, the job we carry out all starts to revolve around drinking.

When we seek pleasure for the sake of pleasure, it leaves us with emptiness (Frankl, 1984), an emptiness that has possibly been there for quite some time now. Alcohol can fill that void, for a period of time, but everytime we become sober we start to feel how things can be so very meaningless.

If life is meaningless, why would we do anything at all? Why go to work? Why not just live day-by-day and have fun drinking?

Eventually, drinking will reduce the amount of dopamine that is transported to your brain. So the only way that you may be able to stay in a state of numbing comfort, would be by being in a constant state of inebriation, we know that this is simply not a sustainable way to live your life. It isn't just about the physical consequences like regular diarrhea, and substantial damage to your liver and gut, but it is also about the fact that it reduces your capability to be happy.

Drinking to chase away your unhappiness or boredom really has the opposite effect on you in the long run.

Discomfort and pain exist in life for a reason. We should not be looking to numb these feelings away. Numbing our discomfort and pain through drinking will make it so we can't become aware of the root causes of our pain and discomfort. We won't be able to learn from life's pains.

Let's take social drinkers as an example. Some social drinkers may have trouble being extroverted and confident about themselves when they are in social situations. Alcohol does a great job at lowering our inhibitions, but we must ask ourselves: when I am sober, why can't I be the same confident and extroverted person I am when I drink? The answer is because to be able to learn new abilities, we have to step outside of our comfort zone, we have to feel discomfort and we have to pay attention to it.

There may be limiting beliefs holding us back from interacting with other people the way we want to. Beliefs such as, 'I am less than these other people,' or ' I don't deserve to be loved, therefore other people are out to harm me.' These types of limiting beliefs are unconscious and if they are not brought to consciousness, they will control our behavior. That is one example of why we need to bring our pains to consciousness, instead of numbing them away by drinking.

Likewise, hiding past trauma and unresolved conflicts from our childhood through alcohol is only treating the symptom and not the root cause. Figuring out what came first, depression or alcohol dependency is much like 'the chicken or the egg' dilemma. Depression can lead to drinking as much as drinking can lead to depression; they are conditions that mutually reinforce each other.

This chapter has been all about trying to discourage you from drinking for different motives. Discouraging you from drinking, however, and in turn encouraging you to pay attention to your pain points is not enough to help you quit. If encouragement and discouragement were enough, there would be no need for this book. You would be able to quit drinking just by receiving support from your family members and friends. Unfortunately, as you may already know, it isn't that easy. That is why we are going to see exactly what it is going to take on your part to be able to take control back of your life.

3

NATURE, NURTURE, AND DRINKING

Every living being is part of a system. We are part of a totality. We are not segregated from our biological and social systems. Each individual is a synthesis between nurture (your environment) and nature (your biological heritage). This is why it is important for you to take into consideration all of the elements in your life when looking at any of your behaviors, including drinking. This concept of looking at the big picture is called holism. A holistic approach just means that we are looking at the whole picture, and trying to understand how every aspect of our life has led us up to the point we are now at.

Nature

In the previous chapter, we talked about how we can be predisposed to alcohol addiction. When you are predisposed to one type of addiction, you are prone to most types of addiction. It is very common to see young people start with alcohol abuse and then move on to different substances or behavioral addictions. Being predisposed to an addiction just means that you have a deficient dopaminergic system. It means that, from the beginning, we have not been producing the amount of endorphins that we should be, and taking a substance would only make our life that much more painful. Like I said, a lack of dopamine production is associated with depression and low levels of motivation. Whether nurture or nature have a larger impact on our lives is a subject of constant debate, so for our purposes we will value them as equals.

Being predisposed genetically does not mean that we are destined for a miserable life. If we are to catch on and become aware of the fact that we have a family history of alcohol abuse and alcohol dependency, then we may change our ways to stop the cycle from propagating. Changes in our lifestyle are usually enough to alter the way in which our brain is electrochemically structured. Some people with more severe cases do have to enter treatment, but for most people, adequate nutrition and an active lifestyle can be enough to offset any predisposition to addiction. Assuming that they do not hinder themselves further by drinking, of course.

Neuroplasticity is the term that refers to the ability each and every one of us has to learn, to adapt, and to change. It is how our brain makes new connections between each neuron. These changes happen when we gain insight, when we become aware of our behavioral patterns, and when we change these patterns, too. Even as adults, we can change our relationship to alcohol and we can change the way we view life. By changing the way we see things, the things we see change. Our paths are not written in stone.

Nurture

There are critical points in our lives that have a large impact on how we see life, and have a large impact on how our brains develop. Our interactions with our family during childhood play a large role. Growing up in an environment affected by alcoholism has profound effects on our development.

The brain of a child raised by alcoholic parents is similar to that of a war veteran. (Selimbasic et. al., 2018; Volpicelli et. al., 1999)

The types of trauma endured by children in alcoholic environments are catastrophic, and this is something we must come to understand. The common factor between these children and war veterans is the high amounts of stress they were exposed to. A constant release of cortisol (the stress hormone) dysregulates the way our brain works. It creates people who have trouble trusting others, people who can't express their feelings openly, and people who are emotionally detached. This is largely due to the abuse and neglect experienced during infancy, experiences which are commonplace when you grow up in an alcoholic environment.

An insecure individual is created by inconsistent and negligent parenting, while aggressive or abusive parenting will create children with a negative outlook on life. When I refer to insecure individuals or individuals who have a negative outlook on life, I mean that the person is not confident, they don't think that everything is going to be ok after a moment of hardship. This outlook makes it so you are not able to internalize a sense of internal security, a feeling that even though things may not look so great right now, they can get better. We are supposed to gain this feeling of safety and security through consistent parenting. Having a bleak outlook on life makes it really difficult to cope with life's frustrations, it makes us see things in black and white. We are not able to see the good when something bad happens. We can't see any other options that lie ahead of our obstacles. Instead, we tend to focus on the bad. This is what it really means to be insecure. A secure individual, on the other hand, can trust that things will be ok, and even in moments of hardship, they can still see all the good in their life.

The distrust and the emotional detachment generated in people who grew up in alcoholic environments has detrimental effects on their ability to socialize. If we constantly distrust the people we interact with, it makes it really difficult to feel safe around them and open up. You are not able to 'let loose' and really just enjoy your social interactions. This is, of course, where drinking comes in since the inhibitions caused by distrust are removed. Instead of dealing with our trust issues, we just drink them away then we find ourselves in a position where we are only able to open up with the aid of alcohol.

You would think that alcoholics are happy people, wouldn't you? Isn't that why we all drink? to be happy? If you have lived with an alcoholic, you may know that this isn't the case.

People think alcohol helps you sleep. It really doesn't. You are sedating yourself when you drink; sedation and sleeping are not the same. Our body needs to fulfill its appropriate sleep cycles in order to feel well-rested and be able to integrate what we learned throughout the day in our memory. When we sedate ourselves we are not entering the deep sleep cycles. We may be getting the quantity of sleep we need, but we are not getting quality sleep. If we are not getting quality sleep, we are not well-rested, leading to a constant state of pessimism and irritability, consequently stress levels increase in our body.

If we take this constant state of irritability and stress and combine it with an inability to feel joy from life's pleasures, we could start to see why violence and alcoholism are so closely intertwined. It makes it really difficult for loved ones to deal with this kind of person. To make matters worse, when you are actually drunk you are removing your inhibitory control. Without inhibitory control, you are not able to regulate your emotions. When we are not able to regulate our emotions or stop ourselves, we get out of control and may act out in a way we normally wouldn't. In normal conditions, we wouldn't physically assault our loved ones, and this is why there is a lot of remorse in people suffering from alcoholism. You see the person apologizing the day after, feeling shame for what they did. The more you drink the more your tolerance increases, making you less sensitive to life's joys, leading to further irritable, depressive, and violent dispositions.

Like the famous psychologist Carl Gustav Jung (1963) once said: If we don't become aware of our shadow, it will control us, and we will project its content onto others. If the alcohol-dependent individual is not self conscious, and does not realize that alcohol is what is making them miserable, they will start to blame others for their misery. They will attribute fault to everything and everybody except themselves or their alcohol consumption. They will say things like, "I have terrible luck," or, "I drink to forget about what a terrible life I have." If you don't bring your own shadow into awareness it will take control of your perception and it will even lead you to project your own negative aspects onto others.

As you can see, it is a cycle. Alcohol leads to unhappy irritable states. These states cause extremely high levels of stress leading the person drinking to be prone to reproduce the pattern they were exposed to. If you are a product of this type of environment, I would invite you to be the one to break the cycle. Especially now that you have gained insight into some of the factors that play a role in AUD, we can start to look at the solutions. In the following chapters we are going to look at what it is we need to do to regain control of our lives, and break the cycle.

4

FROM WILLPOWER AND TEMPTATION TO ACCEPTANCE

The idea that willpower is enough to overcome Alcohol Abuse Disorder (AUD) reinforces the stigma held towards alcohol addiction. As a society we need to understand that AUD should be treated just like any other chronic health condition. You don't go telling somebody who suffers from diabetes that it's their fault for eating too much sugar; you wouldn't go and call somebody suffering from obesity self-indulging and lazy.

Previously, we have believed that obesity was a loss of self control, but now we know that it's in most cases a chronic illness. If we feel that willpower is the answer to quitting alcohol, then we are basically saying that AUD is a moral failing, a sign of weakness, or a lack of willpower. All these ideas just make us feel worse about the fact that we are addicted to alcohol. AUD is not a moral failing, it is a chronic health condition. This is why we have to be able to accept our cravings, and forgive ourselves for having them.Your beliefs about alcoholism need to be altered for you to be able to forgive yourself.

"Your beliefs become your thoughts, Your thoughts become your words, Your words become your actions, Your actions become your habits, Your habits become your values, Your values become your destiny." — Mahatma Gandhi (1868 - 1948)

What would you say to a friend who is feeling shameful for having a drinking problem? What sort of kind and caring words would you have for them?

Now, say those words to yourself.

Our genetics, media, the family we were raised in, and our socioeconomic status growing up are things that we can't change. What we can change is the way we react to these factors. Knowing that something isn't good for you isn't enough to create change. If that were the case then AUD, and tobacco addictions would not be some of the most preventable causes of premature death. One of the main errors lies in the fact that we try to suppress or eliminate our cravings through a sheer display of willpower. We struggle against temptation in a constant tug-of-war. We must be able to forgive ourselves before we can accept our condition.

Acceptance

Acceptance and Commitment Therapy (ACT) has been rising in popularity in recent years, mainly in the fields of addictions and relapse prevention. Detoxing is a necessary first step, but detoxing alone can't assure us long lasting effects. Suppressing cravings can help at first but a rebound effect has been noticed leading to strong relapses. The main reason for the rebound effect is due to our constant use of willpower to suppress cravings. The act of suppressing cravings places a great deal of strain on us, it tires us out. If we become tired, and a triggering event occurs, we are much more susceptible to relapse. This relapse effect correlates with the meta-analysis conducted by Lee et. al., (2015) where they find that the effects of ACT have longer-lasting effects than avoidance and abstinence strategies.

In the same way that you should listen to your pain and discomfort, I suggest that you should also listen to your cravings, instead of tiring yourself out by avoiding your cravings. Avoidance and suppression strategies may work for some, but for the purposes of our work, we will be following the approach proposed by the acceptance and commitment therapy method.

By listening to your cravings and accepting them without passing judgement, we start to create space between ourselves and our cravings, thoughts, and emotions. We stop being overidentified with each internal impulse that rises. When we are overidentified with our cravings we act in an automatic reactionary fashion, similar to the way many animals live: instinctually. An animal gets a craving for water, so it seeks water without questioning itself too much. It is like living on autopilot. We are not governed by our instinctual drives. Instead, we can choose how to react to our own spontaneous thoughts and cravings.

This act of separating ourselves from our cravings, thoughts, and emotions creates an 'observer self.' It creates what we call awareness. If we think of awareness as a muscle, just like any other muscle, it requires exercise. In order to stop living on autopilot we must be able to break our behavioral patterns and create new ones. This ability is inherent to all humans and it is called cognitive flexibility, and it is something we can improve, something we should improve. Somebody who lives on autopilot is easy to control. They are easily controlled by their emotions, cravings, and even by media and external influences.

There are several ways of increasing our awareness and our cognitive flexibility. Any activity that forces you to reassess your previous way of doing things and step outside of your comfort zone will help you. Some of the strongest activities of this kind are creating music, martial arts, yoga, and dancing. Activities like these will snap you out of an automatic way of living. In the following section, I am going to give you an exercise that will strengthen your awareness, and this is an exercise that anybody can incorporate into their routine. It is called diaphragmatic breathing.

Breathwork

- Draw your attention to your breath.
- Breathe in for 4 seconds, making sure you completely fill your lungs. You should be able to raise your chest by doing this.
- Hold your breath for another 4 seconds.
- Breathe out for another 4 seconds.
- Hold the void for 4 seconds.
- Repeat this process 3 to 4 times, or as many times as you feel until you have entered a relaxed state of mind.
- If you wish to hold your breath for longer, you may.

This type of breathing exercise activates your parasympathetic nervous system reducing the intensity with which you feel an emotion or a craving, while at the same time slowing down any thoughts that are racing into your head. If we slow down our thoughts and the intensity of our cravings, it gives us more time to acknowledge and accept them. By practicing this breathing exercise on a daily basis you are going to be training yourself to become more aware of your internal processes. This will create more space between a triggering event and your reaction, and you will be able to redirect yourself, breaking previous behavioral patterns.

We have to accept that it is futile to attempt to avoid all of life's pain and suffering. Avoidance of pain is one of the mains driving forces in any addiction. Acceptance is the opposite of avoidance. Acceptance means choosing to let go of our tendency to avoid. We have generated this avoidance impulse as a defense mechanism that we need to let go of. Instead, we can choose to experience in the present moment the uncomfortable thoughts and feelings that come to us in a compassionate non-judgemental way. Being present involves not lingering too much in the past which can lead to depressive melancholic states, and not focusing too much on the future which leads to excessive feelings of anxiety. Remaining too long in anxious and depressive states raises our cortisol levels which narrows our perception of life. It makes us not be able to see all our actual OPTIONS. We instead develop a black and white way of thinking where we are only able to focus on the negative aspects of our life. Once we have trained ourselves in awareness and cognitive flexibility, we can start to identify and accept our cravings to drink. There is no need to suppress them, instead understand why they come to you when they do and do something about them. This is important so that we can start identifying activating events surrounding our cravings.

Structure, Planning, and Confidence

Not believing in yourself can create a great sense of insecurity. You are worried that something unpredictable and awful is always around the corner. This is due to an underlying belief that we are just going to fail ourselves again. One way to correct this limiting unconscious belief is by planning out our week, and creating a structure to follow. When you say you are going to do something, maybe something as simple as attend a social meeting, you must do so. This will improve how much you trust yourself, and increase your confidence. It's imperative that you stick to your word. Failing to back up your words with actions will only damage the image you have to yourself.

When we are talking about creating a plan we need to take into consideration our activating events that trigger us. Use these following questions to begin to identify your activating events:

Who: Who are the people I associate drinking with?

We want to identify the people around us that stimulate our cravings to drink. Is it a group of friends, is it a family member, or maybe your romantic partner? When it comes to friends, it is important for you to be clear on what your goals are in life. Then we can start thinking about what a friend should be like. Our friends should support us and help us reach our goals, shouldn't they? Or at least accompany us while we figure things out, in both the bad and the good moments of our life.

I am not asking you by any means to stop seeing the people that are important in your life just because they drink. If one of your drinking friends means a lot to you, if they are truly important to you, and you think you are important to them, try to explore what kinds of other things you have in common. See if that person is willing to do other activities with you. Create a common ground that isn't only based on drinking. If the person isn't willing to do anything that doesn't involve drinking, it means you either didn't have much in common, or they're making drinking their top priority. If you feel that their addiction is the problem, forgive them, and give them the time they need to figure things out.

When you stop drinking you realize who your true friends are. Those who will support you, and those who will stick by you, even when it isn't all fun and games. If one of your drinking buddies is a true friend, you will be able to turn the person from a trigger into a support person. That person could be somebody you can ask to help you stop drinking at get-togethers, and could be the person who will help you stay sober, instead of encouraging you to drink.

When it comes to romantic partners it can get much more complicated. The key is to be clear on what your goals and values are. I am going to help you do that in the following chapters. Once your goals and values are clear, you have to ask yourself if the person you're with aligns with your values and goals. Ask yourself if they are willing to make a change. That is if they are in the same type of situation you are in and if they're one of your main triggers. If so, are they willing to make a change? You can't help somebody who doesn't want to help themselves; you can't save them. The best you can do is lead by example.

. . .

What: What does drinking do for me in each particular scenario?

What are you getting out of drinking? Is it boosting your confidence in a social situation? Is it alleviating the emotional and physical pain you feel after a hard day's work? Perhaps you can't sleep, so you just need a quick drink before bed. Understanding what you are getting out of drinking when you get a craving is crucial. If we understand what drinking is doing for us, we can find ways of replacing drinking effectively. It is up to you to figure out what it is doing for you, by practicing awareness, by placing yourself in the observer role.

Some additional questions you can ask yourself are: How are you feeling? Why did the cravings start? What happened that triggered your cravings?

When: Are there time patterns?

This question's objective is to help you see if there is a pattern, if there are certain times during the week or day where your need to drink increases. Maybe it's the end of the day, after work. Perhaps Friday or Saturday night. Maybe cravings arise while you are watching your favorite sporting event. Whatever the time of the day, please record these findings so you can start to notice your own patterns.

Where: Where do we have most of our cravings? Where do we drink?

Do you drink at home? Do you drink when you go to the bar? Or are you drinking everywhere you go?

Please record your findings. When you plan your week, I want you to keep in mind your triggering events. Make a plan that is aligned with the type of change you want manifested in your life. If those triggering events serve you no good, then there is no need for you to place yourself in those situations. You can plan your week around other more fulfilling activities instead.

Identifying these triggers will help you move from living on autopilot to a place of control and empowerment. When a trigger is identified, what behaviors can you use to redirect yourself away from automatically carrying out your desire to drink? What thoughts, what emotions, and what behaviors can you set into motion to replace the desire to drink? The easiest way to replace the existing behavioral patterns is through structure and planning.When using the guide below, try to keep in mind the questions you previously answered and make a list. The goal is to fill your life with activities that align with your goals and values. We will talk about finding your values if those aren't quite clear to you yet. Use the following guide to help yourself plan out the week.

- Plan your meal choices throughout the week, and make them healthier options.
- Create an exercise schedule.
- Set a sleeping schedule.
- Be strict with your work schedule.
- Plan any social meetings that align with your current goals.

Microbiome and Alcohol

The cravings that lead us to drink aren't ours alone. There are microorganisms in our gut that crave ethanol (Singh et. al., 2017). These organisms produce a large amount of dopamine in our body, so they can manipulate our brain's reward centers and send signals that turn into cravings for sugar and alcohol.

Now, let's think about how this happens. Why do we have these pathogenic organisms within us to begin with? We all have them; we are first colonized by bacteria during birth. Most of the bacteria that colonize us are beneficial bacteria that we share a symbiotic relationship with. The ecosystem within our gut is called the microbiome.

Alcohol is used to kill bacteria, this has always been one of its main medical functions. So when we drink it, we decrease the diversity in our gut. When we decrease the diversity of beneficial bacteria in our gut, it allows for opportunistic organisms to reproduce (Dubinkina et. al., 2017).

Usually we have a balanced ecosystem filled with bacteria that protect us from pathogens. Alcohol kills these off, and allows for a genus like Candida Albicans to take control over our food preferences. Drinking alcohol will lead you to have more of these pathogens, and these pathogens will consequently increase your cravings for alcohol (Singh et. al., 2017).

When you have a Small Intestine Bacterial Overgrowth (SIBO), you are prone to conditions such as depression, arthritis, irritable bowel syndrome, and chronic diarrhea. SIBO is the term used to describe the loss of equilibrium inside your gut. This is what happens when you take too many antibiotics or you consume too much alcohol (Francino, 2016; Ohlsson et. al., 2019). You will kill off your good bacteria, losing one of your lines of defense.

Reducing your alcohol consumption is not enough to bring balance to your microbiome. The amount of sugar you consume has to be decreased in general. On average, each individual in the United States is consuming 100 grams of sugar per day (Di Rienzi et. al., 2019). We should be consuming 25 grams of sugar per day, so on average people in the United States are consuming four times the recommended amount. This, of course, leads to SIBO the same way drinking does. Here are some food items to avoid if you wish to restore equilibrium to your gut, consequently reducing your cravings for alcohol while increasing the amount of dopamine that is produced in your gut.

High Sugar Foods:

- Salad Dressing and Most Sauces (BBQ, Buffalo, Ranch, Ketchup, etc.)
- Soda
- Candy
- Tortilla and Potato Chips
- Artificial Juices
- Granola Bars
- Ice Cream
- Breakfast Cereals (Cereals you do choose should have more than 4 grams of fiber and less than 5 grams of sugar per serving)

While sugar feeds the pathogenic organisms within us making them stronger, fiber has the same strengthening effect on our beneficial bacteria. The more fiber we consume, the more our beneficial bacteria kill off the pathogens. They can compete for nutrients with pathogens and starve them to death. I am going to give a few food options that include large amounts of fiber per calorie. Like I said, fiber will help your gut become more biodiverse and will reduce the impact of pathogenic bacteria and consequent alcohol cravings.

Fiber-Rich Options:

- Lentils
- Leafy Greens
- Apples
- Avocado
- Quinoa
- Artichoke
- Sweet Potatoes
- Dark Chocolate

In regards to meat and dairy, there isn't any conclusive evidence that these products directly harm you or your microbiome. The issue with these products is the vast amount of antibiotics farm animals are given in order to produce at optimal levels. Antibiotics are designed to kill bacteria, so it is only natural that excessive consumption of them would impoverish your gut's biodiversity. It is imperative that you know where your animal products are being sourced from if you must eat them (Dudek-Wicher, Junka & Bartoszewicz, 2018).

The suggestion is for you to consume less than 25 grams of sugar and more than 30 grams of fiber per day. This should help you restore the biodiversity in your microbiome, allowing you to have normal levels of dopamine and other endorphins necessary for your emotional regulation. Decreasing the amount of sugar you consume will help mitigate cravings for alcohol, while providing you more room to consume calories that are rich in nutrients.

Physical Activity

When it comes to physical activity, the most important factor is consistency. You don't have to engage in a super intense work-out routine. A 20 minute power-walk will do the job but ramping up the intensity for a 20 minute run instead is even better.

Exercise is painful, and will cause discomfort at first if you are not accustomed to it. The fact that it causes you pain is one of the reasons it helps you regulate the amount of endorphins you produce. The pain you feel from exercise stimulates dopamine production, helping you increase its availability in your body.

Along with the increase in dopamine production, cortisol is also decreased when you exercise. Cortisol is the stress hormone that we talked about. This stress hormone is correlated with high levels of anxiety and depression. If anxiety or depression are some of the triggers that lead you to drink, then exercise should be one of your main focuses.

Sleep Cycles

Sleep disturbances and the consequent effects of sleep deprivation can play major roles in your road to recovery.

People under 30 should be looking to get at least 8 hours of sleep per night. As you get older the amount of deep sleep you require is decreased (Conroy & Arnedt, 2014).

Your sleep cycles function in intervals of 90 minutes; after the first 90 minutes you enter Rapid Eye Movement (REM) sleep. Most of your dreams start to occur in this stage of sleep. In fact, 80 percent of dreams are thought to occur during REM sleep (Payne & Nadel 2002).

Dreams are quite important to our functioning of everyday life. Both dreams and the REM sleep part of the cycle serve as a means to integrate your new experiences into your long-term memory (Payne & Nadel 2002). Basically, you are reinforcing your new pathways in your brain while you are in REM sleep to make sure they are strong enough to recall when we need them.

It has been noticed that when you drink, you don't enter these stages of sleep. That is why I mentioned that even though alcohol sedates you, it doesn't help you sleep (Kotorii et. al., 1980). Dreaming and REM sleep is so important that when you miss out on this sleep stage by drinking, your body actually looks to make up for lost time. A rebound in REM sleep is noticed in people who are experiencing withdrawal symptoms from AUD. When you stop drinking, your body makes up for the lost sleep cycles.

It is hypothesized that this rebound effect in REM sleep is what explains the hallucinations experienced during severe cases of Delirium Tremens (DT). Your body becomes so deprived of dreaming that it begins to force you to dream while you are awake. We have all heard the stories about how sleep deprivation can make you see things, so it does make quite a bit of sense.

You may be getting your eight hours of sleep, but are you getting quality sleep? Or are you usually waking up tired and lethargic?

The recommendation currently lies in getting about 112 minutes worth of deep sleep, which is sleep that doesn't contain a lot of dreaming. Slow wave sleep (SWS) is the deep sleep stage. In this stage of sleep is where inflammation and our bodily tissues are repaired. This is also where most cellular energy is restored. This stage of sleep is heavily shortened in people who are trying to stop drinking (Conroy & Arnedt, 2014).

The breathing exercise I provided you along with physical activity both will help to reduce stress. Lower levels of stress are linked to improved sleeping cycles (SAMHSA, 2014).

Some signs to look out for are:

- Trouble falling asleep: worrying and overthinking.
- Excessive moving during the night: tossing and turning.
- Waking up during the night.
- Daytime sleepiness and lethargy.

If you have trouble falling as sleep, don't just lay in bed tossing and turning. It is recommended to wake up, maybe even get up and do a light activity like reading a book until you are tired once more.

Melatonin is the hormone that primarily regulates our sleep cycles. Taking a melatonin supplement at the same time every night along with the exercises we mentioned can help you set up a sleeping schedule. This is recommended over pharmaceutical options, since sleep medication can become quite addictive as well. Melatonin supplements are not invasive and non-addictive.

As a recap, exercise and sleeping well both contribute to a lower level of stress in your body which will make it easier for you to manage your emotions and your cravings. As far as nutrition goes, you want to reduce the amount of added sugars you are consuming which will reduce your cravings to consume alcohol. This is done by starving the population of Candida Albicans in your gut. The main goal here is to have a structure, and to follow it. This gives you agency over yourself.

When you are aware of your triggering events, plan your schedule and the activities in your week around things that are aligned with your values and goals. The idea isn't to avoid your triggers, but to fill your week with meaningful activities that bring you longer lasting happiness.

Deviating from your schedule and skipping out on some of your tasks can be a warning sign that you can use to your advantage. When you start noticing that you are not doing what you have intended to do, you will know that you are at risk of losing control again. A structure will allow you to notice irregularities in your own behavior a lot faster.

When you come across strong emotions, whether anger, sadness, or happiness, any emotion at an extreme intensity needs to be balanced out. Relapse doesn't occur in bouts of anxiety or depression, a lot of people drink when they are really happy. Again, you need to detach yourself from the emotion, become aware of it, and accept it. Understand why it is there, but don't let the emotions and cravings control you. You can feel them, everybody does, but you don't have to act on them. Here are some methods you can use to remove yourself from high-intensity emotional states and restore equilibrium. This goes for intense cravings as well.

- Cold Shower
- Diaphragmatic Breathing
- Talking to a sober support person
- Work Out/Fitness Routine

All these methods serve the purpose of resetting our brain. We look to slow down any speeding thoughts coming into our mind, additionally reducing the intensity of our emotions and cravings. Like I said, you want to slow down the process so that you have time to accept and monitor yourself without judgement and in a compassionate way. The goal is to not live automatically controlled by our cravings, but instead be able to make conscious decisions that align with your values and goals.

5

ADDRESSING THE ROOT CAUSE

Avoidance is the opposite of acceptance as far as our work goes. Living your life under the impression that you should be looking for happiness and pleasure exclusively is quite dangerous. Feelings and sensations like guilt, loneliness, anger, fear, and pain all have their roles in our lives. They shouldn't be ignored. Not accepting parts of yourself will make those parts of you unconscious and uncontrollable. These seemingly uncomfortable emotions can then become more complex by mixing with limiting beliefs about ourselves, creating what is called a complex.

Complexes are sets of unconscious beliefs we have about ourselves and our environment. A complex is thought to be self-sustaining and semi-autonomous (Jung, 1959). The fact that we have parts of ourselves that become semi-autonomous if we don't accept them is what makes it feel like we are fighting ourselves when we are trying to take control of our lives. You are literally fighting a part of yourself.

Jung's work on the shadow has now been incorporated into clinical and scientific settings through Acceptance and Commitment Therapy. Jung (1959) mentioned that we have to be able to integrate or embrace our shadow, integrate and bring to consciousness the parts of ourselves that we don't accept.

Pain has its obvious reasons for existing. It has always been there to tell us that we are suffering damage of some sort, whether it be physical or psychological. Pain must be listened to just like all the other emotions we are going to refer to in this chapter. There is much to be learned from leaning into discomfort and over-coming your obstacles. In our suffering, we can find strength and meaning.

Let's think about the process of metamorphosis that a caterpillar goes through to turn into a butterfly. When the butterfly is still in the cocoon it has to break free from the cocoon using its newly-formed wings. If somebody were to help the butterfly break free by ripping open the cocoon prematurely, it will hinder the butterfly's ability to fly. The butterfly needs to break free on its own in order to have the strength in its wings to fly (Dass, 1979).

This is a clear example of how obstacles and struggles can provide us with strength and why they should be faced head on and not avoided.

In the previous chapter I had you make a list of your triggers by asking yourself a few questions. In this chapter I want you to think of the emotions that make those triggers effective. We can get mixed up and think that the triggers are the causes. That going to our friend's house is what makes us drink, or that being with our romantic partner is another reason. Those triggers are easy to blame since they are external and visible. The real causes aren't right in front of us which is why we lose sight of them.

Guilt and Shame

A lot of us look to drinking in order to numb the painful sensations that shame brings. Shame is quite different from guilt. When we talk about shame we are referring to a feeling or unconscious belief that convinces us that we are inherently flawed. Shame says that there is something wrong with us, and our failures or shortcomings are evidence of that truth.

Guilt, on the other hand, is the act of taking responsibility for acting in a way that goes against your own values or against your moral code. It's a feeling that helps you draw attention to areas within yourself that require improvement or change.

When we feel shame, our sense of self-worth is under attack. This happens due to our overidentification with our behaviors and thoughts. We previously discussed how being overidentified with your thoughts can lead you to act in an automatic reactionary way. Well, there are other consequences, too.

Being overidentified with our behaviors or our thoughts is what causes us to feel shame instead of guilt. Overidentification in this case means that you think you ARE your thoughts, you think you ARE your mistakes. No separation is being made between you and your mistakes. This is why making a mistake damages your sense of self-worth.

Your sense of self-worth should not be based on any one of your behaviors. We all make mistakes. No matter how many mistakes you make, however, you are still worthy of being loved, you are still worthy of being happy. You decide what your self-worth is.

One critical aspect that marks the difference between making ourselves feel shameful or guilty is the way we talk to ourselves. When we attack ourselves verbally, when we criticize ourselves, the same pathways in our brain are activated as if we were attacked by an external threat such as a predator.

When you criticize yourself, are you providing yourself feedback so you can change your behavior, or are you telling yourself you're inherently bad?

The only way to find out is by creating space between you and your thoughts, by slowing down the speed with which you create these thoughts. This is done by increasing your awareness using the exercises I provided you in the previous chapter.

Anger and Bravery

Anger is usually thought of as a negative emotion, mainly because it arises when we spot a threat, when our goals are obstructed, or even just because of the unpleasant way anger makes us feel. Being annoyed or constantly angry isn't a pleasant sensation. Your heart rate, blood pressure, and cortisol levels all rise. We have talked about how you can become irritable when you drink constantly due to the lack of quality sleep. So it's safe to say that anger causes many drinkers quite a lot of pain which they look to numb their anger instead of listening to it and addressing the root cause.

This emotion has always helped us protect ourselves from predators by placing us in the kill or be killed state. It's responsible for the 'fight' in the fight-or-flight response. The release of acetylcholine and adrenaline during states of anger makes it so we are ready to act, and become focused on our target. Acetylcholine regulates our ability to focus, we wouldn't want to be distracted by a flock of birds flying by while we're being attacked by a predator.

Taking into consideration that anger can make us ready to act and help us narrow our sights on our targets gives us a clue on how we might be able to use anger to our advantage. The fact that it helps us focus on the areas of life we feel we should change is one of anger's main functions.

Being angry at yourself or at life for the set of circumstances you have been dealt is normal. What you decide to do with this anger is up to you, though.

Anger is meant to help us deal with our obstacles. It is a way of helping us harness the initiative necessary to be brave enough to create a change in our lives.

Anger turned inwards can lead to feelings of self-loathing, feelings that can turn into suicidal tendencies if they're not brought to awareness and dealt with. If you are experiencing these sorts of thoughts, and at times you feel like you just don't want to continue because you are unable to forgive yourself for your mistakes, I want you to take this following reflection into consideration.

When you want to commit suicide, you really just want to kill the current person you are. You are able to change. You don't really want to kill yourself, you want to be reborn. Myths of rebirth are present in most, if not all, cultures. One of the most popular ones is that of the phoenix, a bird that dies only to be reborn from its own ashes, becoming stronger each time it dies.

These small deaths, existential crises, or emotional breakdowns we experience aren't pleasant by any means, but they provide the opportunity for you to reinvent yourself. Once you bring that awareness to recognize that anger is at the root of drinking, you can use anger's initiative and focus to create change in yourself and in your life.

Don't ignore your anger: it's trying to tell you something. It's trying to tell you that you think that something isn't fair or just in your life, and that you want to create change. The best part is, anger can be turned into passion for justice, the passion required to defend and protect those you love, including yourself. It gives you the initiative to set things right!

Something to keep in mind is that anger usually arises as a secondary emotion. It is born out of shame or fear first, in most cases. An example of this is when you are driving. Let's say another driver runs a red light and puts your life at risk. You slam the brakes, a reaction fueled by fear, but quickly enough your fear turns into anger when you realize just how inconsiderate and unfair that person was with you.

When anger is born out of shame, it means that your sense of self-worth might not be internally rooted. Perhaps you are not able to take criticism well from others because it makes you feel like you are flawed, so you develop a need to always be right. This all stems from placing your sense of self-worth on what others think. Accepting the fact that you can make a mistake or that you can be wrong sometimes while knowing that you are not worth less for being imperfect really helps stabilize your sense of self-worth. Perfection doesn't exist. The beauty of imperfection is that there is always room to change, and grow. You can always change and grow, so don't let a single one of your mistakes make you think otherwise. You are not your mistakes; you are not inherently bad.

The anger that arises usually matches the intensity with which you felt afraid or shameful. This may help you understand the underlying causes of your anger or annoyance a bit better.

Fear and Anxiety

Fear has proven quite useful to us in an evolutionary sense. It is responsible for the 'flight' aspect in the fight-or-flight response, allowing us to secrete adrenaline to help us escape predators.

Fear has many manifestations in our social reality. One of the most popular forms of fear that people who drink suffer from is anxiety; that they have constant worries about the future.

Ignoring or avoiding our fears means that we don't realize what is actually fueling them. There are two factors behind our fears.

First, our fears are born out of needs that we have. Basic human needs such as the need to feel safe, or the need to belong and be accepted. Fears, however, are not simply expressions of our needs; they are distorted versions of our needs.

The second factor that distorts the expression of our needs are the unconscious limiting beliefs we have about ourselves. These beliefs tell us we are not worthy, therefore, our needs won't be met unless we do something about it. With this last statement you can see that if we are unsure or we feel insecure about how the world may treat us, we will develop a need to control our outcomes.

Control is born out of a fear associated with uncertainty. Uncertainty is unavoidable in life, we don't have control over most things in life. We don't decide what socioeconomic status we are born into, or even what our genetic heritage is made up of. Like Frankl (1984) says, there are sociological, biological, and psychological factors in life that we don't have any control over, but we do have a single freedom. It's the freedom to choose our attitude towards the conditions that life imposes on us.

Freedom comes with great responsibility. It's the responsibility of giving your life a meaning, sometimes taking advantage of the hand of cards you have been dealt, and other times in spite of it (Frankl, 1984).

So if what we *can* control is our attitude towards the things that happen to us, how could this help us deal with our fears, with our anxiety?

There are a few ideas and feelings that we must internalize in order to react to the circumstances that life assigns us in a different way. First, we have to work on our outlook on life, our expectations and predictions about how others and our environment operate. The feelings or ideas we should look to internalize are those of trust, in our selves and in the universe, while also being present.

Our sense of security directs the way we expect our environment to treat us. If we're excessively worried about the possible outcomes of our life, it means we fear that we may not like what life has in store for us. This way of looking at life makes it really difficult to cope with life's struggles. In a moment of hardship, if you don't trust the world you live in, you will fall into depression, and it will lead to feelings of wanting to give up.

The difference between depression and sadness is a matter of perspective. We all experience sadness, but people who are sad still remember all the good in their lives, they know that even though things are not ok at the current moment, they will be ok again. They understand this since they have overcome other struggles in their lives. A depressed individual does not trust his environment, so he will be filled with feelings of hopelessness.

Think back to when you didn't drink. I want you to remember one of the most difficult times in your life. What helped you overcome it?

The key here is to stop seeing life in black and white terms or to stop seeing things as all good or all bad. Your emotions aren't all good or all bad. There are a lot of grey areas. Many people realize this in early stages of development, but others don't. Accepting others and yourself with their flaws helps you accept the discomfort of life's struggles.

Practice Feeling Grateful

Not being able to see the good in yourself makes it easy to fall into depressive states, while not being able to see the actual options you have in your life and only focusing on your problems can make you terribly anxious. Each morning when you wake up, try to think of three things you are grateful for. Be grateful about an aspect of yourself, be grateful for having somebody else in your life, and be grateful for a general aspect of your life. Doing this right when you wake is useful, since this is the time of day where we have the most cortisol in our body. The stress hormone is released in our body and is at its peak during the morning so that we leave the comfort of our bed and wake up.

The most important part about gratitude is **experiencing** or **feeling** the sensation. Gratitude helps reduce your psychological stress levels and improves your quality of sleep (Seligman, Steen, Park &Peterson, 2005). Expressing gratitude helps achieve a general state or mood of being grateful which creates changes in your brain's chemistry. It really doesn't matter whether you are grateful to god, nature, the universe, yourself, or society. You just need to generate that feeling within yourself.

That is why I recommended that you try being grateful first thing in the morning and the last thing at night. Some people have the habit of reflecting upon their day or even their life right before they go to bed. This is fine, since we can review our behavior during the day in a more emotionally detached manner and provide ourselves constructive criticism about how we handled things but we should limit how long we do this for. There is the danger of getting stuck in a mental loop, going over the same situations again and again.

I've gotten stuck in repetitive thinking patterns at night in the past. One night I decided to try to force myself to be grateful in that precise moment. I was skeptical when I tried it. I didn't believe it would help the way it did. When I started, the tightness around my brain felt like it was released. It was like relaxing a constricted muscle. My mind became more open to other thoughts and options.

I urge you to try feeling grateful while you are having an anxiety attack, or while you are having looped in negative, repetitive thinking patterns that don't let you sleep.

In order to trust yourself, you have to be aware of your strengths and limitations while being grateful for both.

Write down two strengths you have and two limitations in your life. Find something good about the limitations, note a way in which they have helped you grow. Practice feeling grateful about them. Keep your strengths and limitations present at all times.

Gratitude along with a structured way of life will help you gain trust in yourself and will make you feel a real sense of safety. Trust in yourself and trust in the way your environment is going to treat you. Having this general sense of trust and confidence really changes the way you relate to your fears and the way you perceive your obstacles.

The second concept that we must internalize, so that we are not controlled by our fears is 'being present.' Anxiety can be thought of as too much future, while depression can be thought of as too much past (Dass, 1979). This takes us back to not living on autopilot. When we are on autopilot, we are easily controlled by our fears since we automatically act in accordance with our previous experiences and our expectations about the future.

To help you get an idea of how the unconscious mechanisms work, let's think of an everyday scenario that most of us have witnessed if not experienced directly. When you went to school, did you ever call your teacher, "Mom?" If you didn't, maybe somebody in your class did. It was always amusing and the whole classroom would burst in laughter when it happened.

This occurred because we have a tendency to transfer our emotions from one situation to the next. It is a normal function that all humans have. Perhaps you saw or felt a few similar qualities in your teacher as you saw in your mother. A nurturing, authoritative female figure which evoked the same types of feelings you had around your parents. We have a tendency to fill in the blanks of what we perceive in each situation by using our previous experiences and our expectations about the future.

What do you see in the following figure?

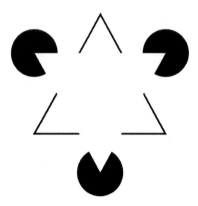

Many answers are provided when I ask this question. Some people report one triangle being in front of three circles and another triangle in the back. The truth is there isn't a single triangle in the figure. Our brain fills in the triangles using its expectations about how we think the physical universe works.

Take this same concept and apply it to social interactions. When we meet somebody, how much of that person are you actually seeing? How much of what you see is just you filling in the blanks with your prejudices and assumptions? Being present in the moment is all about catching yourself. Making sure you are not attributing characteristics to people and situations which are not really there.

Prejudices can be manipulated by media and society through subliminal influences, as we have previously discussed. This is why it's so important to take a moment and create some space between you and your thoughts, so that you are not controlled by your prejudices. This act of creating space allows you to be flexible, it allows you to adapt to each situation, to be present and act in accordance to your values, not your fears.

Sadness and Depression

We have discussed the difference between sadness and depression, sadness helps us find our way, while depression traps us.

Feeling sad is another way in which our body tells us that we should make amends, that we should make up for what has been lost. Loss is the main factor that fuels sadness. The loss of a loved one is a particularly strong cause of sadness (Wolpert, 2008).

Sadness within us looks to bring us together. Let's think about loneliness for a moment. Loneliness is an expression of sadness. From an evolutionary point of view, if we were separated from our tribe, it would probably be a good idea to feel discomfort, to feel a need to get back to them. This would prevent us from getting singled out by a predator. Unity and connectedness are the underlying needs that are not being met when we feel sad.

Loneliness and loss of connection are very prominent reasons for why we drink, but drinking numbs the emotions, it doesn't satisfy the need for connection in a very long lasting manner. Drinking out of loneliness is an indicator of just how much you value *love* and *attachment* in your life. It's showing you that one of your core values is finding people to connect with.

If you realize this is one of your core values, then instead of drinking, you should be fitting time in your schedule to plan activities that bring you closer to the people you care about, closer to making meaningful connections with people you share common interests with. You can feel lonely even when you drink with your friends. If that is happening, then you have to understand that your needs are not being met in the current social circles you are in.

We talked about how sometimes the only thing we have in common with the people we drink is drinking! This fact is what makes you continue to feel lonely or disconnected.

Another way that sadness helps us create a feeling of connectedness is through empathy. When we go through struggles and suffering, it makes it easier for us to understand other's pain as well. It allows us to be compassionate, and not feel like we are alone in our suffering.

Lacking empathy may occur if we don't feel our sadness. If we numb our sadness, it can create a feeling of segregation. You start to feel alone and this feeling of being abandoned creates trust issues. We have talked about how not trusting others creates a negative outlook on life. This negative outlook, the loss of connection and trust is what allows sadness to turn into depression (Fido & Richardson, 2019).

During severe bouts of depression you will feel like there is no way out, no solution. You don't believe life has anything good in store for you, and that you won't recover. Increasing your levels of empathy can increase how connected you feel to nature, how connected you feel in general which can help you trust the world, and feel less lonely (Fido & Richardson, 2019).

To increase your levels of empathy, you can take on new tasks, difficult tasks, and leave your comfort zone. For example, I decided to learn a new language because I wanted to be more understanding of immigrants from Spanish speaking countries, my partner at the time was also learning Spanish. I wanted to understand the struggles they were going through when they moved to a new country. As I learned a new language, I realized just how insensitive I could be with others' struggles.

Feeling connected and having a general sense of security allows you to recover from great losses. Connection keeps you from falling deeply into depression through feelings of not being alone and knowing that things can get better.

Depression and alcohol use disorders go hand in hand. In fact, 50 percent of individuals that are treated for AUD also show signs of major depressive disorders (Riper et. al., 2013). Dysregulation in the dopaminergic systems is present in both alcohol abuse and depressive disorders which is one of the reasons they frequently coexist within an individual.

Drinking and depression reinforce and intensify each other. One of the ways drinking can lead to depression is by damaging our sense of self-worth. When drinking starts to interfere with our priorities and the decisions we make, we might find ourselves choosing to go out for some drinks knowing we may put at risk our professional and academic integrity. We start calling in sick to work, or we may stop doing our school work on time. We start to let others down, but more importantly, we let ourselves down. The inconsistencies between our goals and our actions start to add up, and we stop being able to trust ourselves, to believe in ourselves. A general feeling of disappointment shrouds us.

Our relationships suffer the same fate. They start being a second priority, and we begin to lose connection with some of the people who are most important to us.

We lose sight of our goals and we lose touch with the meaningful relationships that fill us with joy. Loss is the key theme here. We begin to feel sad about all the things that we lose. We don't trust ourselves anymore because we keep failing ourselves through our inconsistent behavior. We start to feel like we are inherently weak or bad, like there is no hope of things getting any better. This is how drinking can lead to depression.

The worst part is that we then begin to drink to drown our sorrows, and we get stuck in an endless self-destructive cycle. Society begins to reject you, you lose your job, you lose your wife or husband, you lose the beautiful relationship you had with your son or daughter. As we know, humans have a need to belong, a need to feel accepted, a need to feel connected. Without having these needs met, we will always feel like there is something missing, like there is a hole we are trying to fill. We look to fill that emptiness by turning on the TV and having another beer.

The second reason drinking can lead to depression is due to its biological consequences. Alcohol is a depressant: you may feel uplifted at first but in the long-term you are decreasing certain functions in your brain that are tied to your ability to feel content (Riper et. al., 2013). Serotonin and dopamine receptors in your brain become damaged and make you experience less joy in your day-to-day life.

People who are biologically predisposed to depression also have a hard time producing the chemicals required to feel happy and to enjoy the simple pleasures in life. A healthy lifestyle, however, can definitively ameliorate these conditions. The problem is that drinking only makes matters worse. Depression is largely genetic, as are alcohol use disorders. If you are predisposed for one, you are more likely to suffer from the other as well (Riper et. al., 2013).

The most dangerous part about the interaction between drinking and depression is suicide. About 37 percent of successful suicides are related to drinking problems (Conner et. al., 2014).

We know that alcohol is considered a disinhibitor, so when we drink while we're having suicidal thoughts, we may do things we wouldn't normally do when we're sober. People may act upon their suicidal thoughts when they are in this disinhibited state.

Some of the same methods that we discussed for reducing stress and increasing your brain's functions can be used against depression as well. For example, studies show that robust cardiovascular exercise does decrease depressive symptoms. Specifically, 45 minutes three times a week of jogging or other more intense physical activities can reduce stress and improve outlook (Cicek et. al., 2015).

As far as mindfulness goes, this has also shown great promise in helping with depression.

I would recommend a combination of both mindfulness and exercise. There are two art forms that are known for this. Taichi, a Chinese martial art, is great for all ages. It's physically demanding but it isn't harsh on your body. The art is about channeling your 'chi' or your life energy while being mindful of yourself and your movements. It's a way to meditate while moving. The other recommendation is Yoga which holds similar characteristics. Both of these art forms have grown in popularity and have become extremely accessible to all.

I taught you how to do diaphragmatic breathing in the previous chapter. Now, let's take it one step further.

First, run the diaphragmatic breathing exercise I gave you three times.

- Sit in a comfortable position, breathing normally, for five minutes without creating a thought.
- Notice that thoughts come to you. Even when you are not actively creating any thoughts, even when you are trying to leave your mind blank.
- Don't suppress the thoughts. Allow them in, and just observe.
- Watch these thoughts without passing judgement.
- You can ask your thoughts, "Why have you come to me at this moment?"

Meditation is great for your long-term improvement. If your depression is really severe, then you may want to consult a physician so that they can find the right combination of medication and psychotherapy for you to stabilize. In most cases, however, people can find their own way to healing with a little guidance and insight of course.

Like I mentioned previously, depression is a symptom of seeing life in black and white terms, of not being able to remember all the good in your life, of not being able to remember your goals and ambitions during your struggles. There is a biological component to depression, but we can act in spite of our biology. The chemical composition in your brain can be changed by your thoughts, and by your beliefs (Rossouw, 2013). The fact that your brain has a current chemical composition does not mean you're destined to be depressed or addicted your whole life. This is the danger of using labels. People tend to blame their biological constitution for their life, not taking responsibility for the life they have created.

Talking to somebody about your problems and seeing them in a new light can change the chemical composition of your brain. It's not set in stone (Rossouw, 2013).

I want to emphasize the fact that we must take responsibility for our life. We can't go around blaming our genetic make-up, the socioeconomic status we were born into, or others for the things that happen to us. In the end, you decide what you do with the hand of cards you have been dealt. Many people are born predisposed to depression and alcohol use disorders, but a lot of these people are able to overcome their genetic predispositions. We are not just the products of our environment and our genetics.

This fact that people don't take responsibility for themselves makes it extremely difficult for them to apologize for their behavior. This is due to the automatic fashion in which they live life. A person can't apologize for their behavior if they can't even recognize it to begin with.

I do want to help you reestablish your relationship with drinking and with your emotions, so that you don't just quit, but also find your path in life. The idea is to make changes in your life that will make you want to stay healthy. Fill yourself with a purpose.

Happiness and Mania

I have talked about how seemingly negative emotions aren't all bad, right? The same goes for happiness and pleasure: it isn't all good. We will continue with the idea of not seeing things in black and white, of seeing the good in the bad and the bad in the good. This concept is ancient, it is expressed by the Yin and Yang. Too much of a good thing is still too much. The difference between poison and medicine is the dose. This phrase can help you understand the concept of equilibrium that I am trying to express to you.

People don't only relapse or lose control of their drinking behaviors when they are angry or sad. People also lose control when they are drinking during times of extreme happiness, as a form of celebration.

There is a famous story about George Best, the professional winger for the Manchester United football team. He was suffering from AUD, and he sobered up after having a liver transplant. He went one whole year without drinking, so he decided to celebrate. He celebrated by having a few drinks, and then six months later he died due to liver failure. Needless to say, he continued drinking after his celebration. This is an extreme example, but cases like these are quite common.

To get a good idea about how being too happy or too confident can also be risky when trying to gain control over yourself, we should look at some more extreme cases.

Bipolar personality disorder is one of the most diagnosed conditions in our times. This may be because we all have our ups and downs. Everything that goes up, must come down, just like the pendulum swings left with the same force we used to move it to the right. Individuals that suffer from bipolar disorders aren't people who feel happy one minute and then sad the next. A person with this condition may feel extremely confident or happy for a whole week, in what is called a 'manic state' and then the next two weeks they can be severely depressed.

When a person is in a manic state, they may feel more extroverted and overly confident. This can lead them to spend a little more money, socialize in inappropriate ways, and do things that they wouldn't normally do if they weren't in this elated state. Cheating on a spouse or partner is a common occurrence during these states. Manic states paired with the loss of inhibition provided by drinking can lead to very questionable decisions. During manic states, it is easy to imagine that people will go out and drink more often, mainly to celebrate how great they feel.

After the person acts upon their heightened state of 'happiness' in a reckless fashion, they may begin to feel shameful about all the things that they did. They start to feel bad about themselves and become depressed. In the depressed state the person loses motivation and stops doing a lot of things. They may become uninterested or unable to carry out their obligations because of how depressed they are. They may even continue to drink to chase away their shame. Then they might start to feel ashamed about all the things that they are NOT doing. What follows is a need to overcompensate, to start to try to get up and feel better, to go back to a manic state. Shame is the driving factor of this cycle. Bipolar disorder is very common among people who drink since it fits right into their lifestyle of extremes.

There are extreme cases, and we can all learn from these. We all carry these characteristics within us to some degree, so being mindful of patterns is important even if the ups and downs aren't so extreme.

Next time you need a drink, pause for a moment and imagine what it would be like not to have the drink. What do you feel? What if you were to allow yourself to feel that way? Listen to the feeling. See why it has come to you.

6

REPLACING PLEASURE WITH MEANING

When I asked you to plan out your week, I didn't ask you at any point to avoid your triggers. Instead, the goal was to REPLACE those activities with more meaningful and fulfilling activities that align with your values. The idea is for you not to focus on quitting alcohol, but to focus on creating change in your life and finding meaning in it.

Abstinence should not be our goal. Finding meaning in our lives is the goal. Abstinence is the side-effect of finding a purpose. Your purpose can be looked at as the sum of your values, and the interactions between them.

What are your values?

Before you are able to efficiently create structure in your life, you must replace your previous behavior patterns with actions that align with your values. This can only be done once you have identified your triggers and your underlying unseen causes.

Your values must be clear to you, clear to the point that you could recall them whenever somebody asks you about them. This is how you will know what kind of activities to plan your week around, consequently detoxing yourself.

There are common values amongst people. Some of the more common ones are connection, adventure, challenge, creativity, and equality (Harris, 2009). If you value adventure, that's fine, it's a common value that people have. It's the need to find or create new and stimulating experiences. It's important for you to be aware of that need, and don't ignore it. Find time in your week to engage in new activities: develop a new hobby, meet new people, or visit a new place. The need isn't going to go away on its own, so become aware of it and make a plan to satisfy it.

You don't have to wait to be completely detoxed to begin to find your purpose. Use your values as a roadmap. Bringing in new activities to your life and reconnecting with your true friends and loved ones in meaningful ways will automatically push aside your need to drink.

Detoxing is going to be one of the most difficult moments in recovery. You're most likely to be sleep deprived and perhaps malnourished, making for an irritable and fragile emotional disposition. As you begin to sober up, your sense of responsibility is going to kick in and the feelings of shame and guilt can easily become overwhelming, taking you towards depression. Motivation is hard to find when you're depressed, but with a decent sleep schedule, some emotional support and a healthy diet, this phase should be temporary.

Regular physical activity will increase your tolerance to discomfort. Anytime you set a goal, you should aim to surpass it while you're exercising to meet it. It's important to surpass your goal so each time you can also increase your threshold to discomfort and increase your endurance.

This will translate into being able to handle more discomfort and stress in your everyday life, since the chemicals in your brain that are released during exercise are the same that will make you feel discomfort during unpleasurable moments of your life. You also have a feeling of accomplishment when you beat what you have done previously whilst working out. Small wins.

Remember, the real danger lies in blaming our depression, blaming the system, blaming our family. This type of attitude can easily turn to giving up, since you are programming yourself to believe that you don't have any agency/control over the things that happen to you.

Then the question is, how do we know we're on the right path?

Sometimes we lose sight of our values and consequently our goals. We lose our direction in life. This is mainly because we don't have our values well defined, or maybe the priorities among our values aren't clear to us on a daily basis. People don't give equal importance to their values, each person's value hierarchy is constituted differently.

People may go to college because that is what is expected of them, or because they think that's what you are supposed to do. Without self-reflection, some people have never stopped and wondered why it is they do what they do.

In previous times we really didn't need to think for ourselves, so we didn't have this issue. We were told what was important by different institutions such as the state or the church. In medieval times, thinking and choosing your own values was not well received. You were given a path to follow, you were told what was right and what was wrong. Making your own path could even be considered heresy, so it was quite dangerous.

Socioeconomic status also determined what path you followed in the past. If you were born a peasant or in a low caste (social stratus system) you were supposed to know your place, and you should know what to aspire towards. You were even told how you should behave, so there wasn't that much thought needed about what path to take.

In our modern era, these control mechanisms have lost a lot of their power. We feel we're free to choose our path for the most part. Freedom comes with a great responsibility though. You are responsible for creating your own path. There are so many options, and so many paths to choose from, that some people feel overwhelmed and lost in an ocean of possibilities.

Happiness isn't pleasure alone. It also isn't the absence of pain or sorrow. Happiness is a conscious choice to appreciate the good in spite of the bad, it's sticking by your values, it's standing by what you find important in life. It's not perfection that we're after.

Values

Values are our freedom, our liberty to choose one life-style over another. They help us decide and prioritize. Values are hierarchical in nature, so you may find some more important than others which is why you are able to make decisions.

We are going to use Dr. Viktor Frankl's (1955) categories to better understand how values can be expressed. Frankl was a Jewish psychiatrist who was taken into concentration camps during WWII and survived. He gained much insight through the suffering he experienced and witnessed in the concentration camps.

The first category provided by Frankl includes creative values, things that you create or do. This is what people mean when they say they want to make a difference or leave a mark in the world. Perhaps you value equality, so you look to create a charitable business or foundation to help those in adverse circumstances. Some people find a meaning in their life through science, religion, creating art, or simply by making a difference in the life of those they hold dear. This creative action is the realization of your potential.

The second category is of experiential values. These are values focused on the receptivity of experience. We wish to experience love, oneness with nature, behold the beauty of art and the astonishment of science. We live to experience what the world has in store for us and appreciate all its wonders.

The third category is a bit more complex, and usually we only resort to thinking about it in the darker moments of our lives. It's called the attitudinal values.

Frankl (1984) was stripped of everything in life: he lost his family, his career, his home, and even his freedom when he was taken into the concentration camps. He didn't have any control over his life at that point. Values related to creating or experiencing couldn't be pursued. If everything is taken away from you, what do you have left?

Your attitude towards your experiences is the only true freedom you have in life.

The way you look at your struggles and the attitude you hold towards the limitations life places on you has substantial effects on the experience and outcome of a situation. Frankl (1984) noticed how some people in the concentration camps fell ill and died more quickly than others. He asked himself why this happened. What marked the difference between those who survived and those who didn't? As a psychiatrist he started to look for behavioral patterns, and he noticed that not too long before the individual would fall ill, they would first tend to suffer from a case of 'give-up-itis.' He would notice that once a person gave up, once they didn't see a point to all their suffering, soon after they would often fall ill and die.

If you don't have a reason to live, if you look at life's struggles as pointless pain, it's going to make it extremely difficult for you to overcome suffering.

Why do you want to recover? What for?

Why are you even reading this book?

Attitudinal values are the ways we react to life's limitations. Such limitations include time, death, and genetics. A lot of people aren't fully aware of the unchangeable aspects of their lives until perhaps a loved one passes away, or they are diagnosed with a terminal illness. In these moments is the realization that your only freedom is how you wish to interpret and react to the situation, your only freedom is your attitude towards life's struggles.

Alternatively, finding meaning in your suffering and being able to use it to grow, to learn, will help you bounce back from the most atrocious and unfair conditions.

There are no right or wrong answers when it comes to values. You choose them. They can't be given to you. What I can give you, however, is a guide that can show you how to prioritize your values. Let's say you value wealth and financial success, but if you fall ill you can't really pursue financial success for very long. The same is true that while you value experiencing love, health is still a requirement.

Here is a pyramid of needs constructed by Abraham Maslow to help you prioritize some of your values. This is a pyramid of basic needs which fuel our values. Basic needs must be met first before we are able to transcend ourselves and do something that's greater than ourselves. Before you are able to help anybody else, and fulfill your need to contribute to society, you have to ask yourself, have I helped myself? Have I helped my family? Have I helped my neighborhood? You must first start by accepting and loving yourself before moving forward and pursuing something greater than yourself.

There is one more distinction I would like to make. Sometimes when I ask people to name their values, they may say things like 'work' or 'family,' and it's understandable since these can be really important aspects of our lives. Work and family, however, are means by which we attain what is important to us, by which we fulfill our needs. If we value love and connection then our family can help us attain that; they can help us attain a sense of belonging as well. If we value putting in effort to help our family and to progress professionally, then work can give us that. Work and family are the means by which you attain what is valuable to you, not the values themselves.

To find the underlying value ask yourself, What does *family* do for me? What am I getting out of this? This question should allow you to find out what the underlying need you value is.

. . .

Make a list of your values.

Write down five values related to things you want to **create or do** in your life.

Write down five values related to things you would like to **experience** in your life.

Order all 10 values from most important to least important.

Base your weekly plan around the most important values you have. Make sure that you're spending more time and energy on activities that align with those values.

Now, answer the following question:

What meaning do you give to your suffering? How have the painful experiences you've been through helped you grow?

Let me give you an example. I feel that my struggle with alcoholism has helped gain the insight and motivation needed to reach out to others and help them through their process. I feel that I would not be the same person without the pain and struggles I have gone through.

Now I want to clarify that if you can change a situation for the better, you should. Changing your attitude to life's pains only applies if you can't create any sort of change in your life, if things are outside your control. If you can create change and you don't do anything, that's a whole other story. That's called masochism.

If you are having trouble finding some of your values, answer this question.

Think back to one of the most difficult moments in your life, what helped you get through it?

Can it help you get through your drinking problem, too?

Drinking can rise quickly in the list of our priorities, mainly because it can help us temporarily meet a lot of the needs we value, like the need to connect, the need to feel accepted, and the need for adventure.

Alcohol use disorders may have their biological predispositions, but the underlying factor that leads to addiction is a person's outlook on life. We all have a tendency to search for meaning. If we don't find meaning in our sober life we will look for other routes. We will look to escape this pointlessly painful existence. Meaninglessness and nihilism eventually lead you to believe that you don't have much to live for, an extremely dangerous and depressing idea.

It has been noticed that this existential void we speak of occurs when we follow somebody else's values and a way of life that has been picked out for us. We're born into a world created by others, after all, and we may look externally for our values and emotional validation, allowing the world to tell us where we belong, and where we fit.

This reliance on the external world for our values occurs due to a lack of introspection and reflection. You must take the time to think about what it is you want and what it is you need. Society's formula for happiness doesn't apply to everybody. You have to find your own path.

This is partly why you see people that are unhappy at their jobs and in unhappy marriages. It's because they aren't being true to themselves. They're trying to live up to the expectations their parents had of them, expectations they feel society has of them. What does it mean to be successful and happy?

Is happiness going to college, getting a job, and having children? Is that success? It may be to some but not all of us. When we lack self-awareness, we end up living on autopilot doing things because that's the way we're supposed to do things. We end up not questioning ourselves too much, relying externally for our sense of direction, for our sense of purpose.

Living up to externally imposed values is one factor that leads to existential emptiness in life, the second is pursuing pleasure and happiness. Pursuing pleasure and happiness for the sake of pleasure and happiness will cause the opposite effect. This is called the Hedonic Paradox.

I will talk to you about sex and its role in a monogamous relationship to better understand how the Hedonic Paradox works. Let's say your goal in sex is to experience an orgasm, meaning that you look to sex as a means to obtain pleasure directly. Each time you have sex with your partner, you're programming your brain to see your partner as an object by which you obtain pleasure. The satiation people feel after an orgasm can give us a clue as to how and why people become bored of their romantic partner. After an orgasm, sometimes people don't even want to be touched, they act as if they 'got what they wanted' as the feeling of satiation sets in. This repeated satiation eventually makes you feel bored in your relationship. Seeking pleasure for the sake of pleasure leaves us with an existential emptiness, and boredom is one of the key indicators that we are living our lives in a pleasure-centered manner. Looking to avoid pain and seek pleasure is the purpose of people living this way. This type of interaction can help explain the ever growing divorce rates in our modern era.

Like with any other object or drug, we gain tolerance to its pleasurable effects. As time goes on we receive less and less pleasure from the object, which makes us have to consume more of it, or look for this same pleasure in other activities or people. On the other hand, if your goals towards sex is bonding and expressing appreciation for your partner, things can play out differently. Through bonding and appreciation of each other, an orgasm and pleasure should be the side-effect of a meaningful interaction, not the goal itself.

For the pleasure seeker, the question becomes, "How much pleasure can you (or it) give me?" Once a person or an object loses its capacity to provide that pleasure, or provide as much pleasure as it once did (an inevitable circumstance), then the object or person loses its value and is discarded for something that promises to be more pleasurable (Nakken, 1999).

In this same regard, directly pursuing happiness or wealth can result in a much more difficult task than it should be. Following your purpose and surrendering yourself to what life has in store for you, doing something greater than yourself will bring wealth and happiness as side-effects. This is why it's so important to believe in the work that you do day-to-day. You must give your struggle a meaning. Otherwise, it can become so unbearable that we need to find a way to sedate ourselves at the end of the day.

Our goal here is not only to recover from addiction, but restore meaning and excitement to your life, so that the needs that you meet through drinking can be met through longer lasting fulfillment. I don't want you to change your behavior, but to look within yourself. Change in your behavior will come as a side-effect of reuniting with your purpose, from looking inwards.

Frankl (1984) mentions that we can't understand alcohol addiction without the term existential vacuum. This is a term used to describe a lack of meaning in a person's life. When we don't act in accordance with our values, and we don't meet our underlying needs, we get this sense of existential emptiness. The existential vacuum is a painful experience that we look to chase away by searching for pleasure, but we only fill that emptiness momentarily.

You may feel like something is missing, life may seem boring, and that's because you are missing a purpose, a meaning.

Pleasure and happiness should not be sought out for themselves. They are side-effects of living a meaningful life, of acting in accordance with your values.

Rising above your suffering and not playing a victim to biology and society is what is going to generate change in your life.

When you are creating the structure we talked about in the previous chapter, don't look to avoid the activities that trigger you. Instead, focus on including activities that bring you closer to the values you have written down. Those activities will be far more meaningful to you.

Part of the issue in recovery lies in the fact that when you use drinking to numb your pain, you lose out on learning other effective coping strategies. We should all develop healthy coping mechanisms for dealing with pain and life's struggles.

You already know what lies down the path of addiction, so why not find out what happens when you choose to align with your purpose? Why not find out when you choose to follow a different path?

Structure can help rebuild the pathways in our brain that we associate with feeling like we are on the right path. When we drink, all our coping mechanisms become associated with drinking. We train our brain to know what to do when we are feeling anxious, depressed, angry, shameful, or happy. You know that the answer to each situation is drinking. This is what the latin root for addiction (addictus) means. It was a term that references the idea of a slave. In our context it means to be a slave to a single coping mechanism. That has helped you deal with life for so long that it becomes the only answer to life's struggles.

Through the plan that I am proposing to you, your brain will recognize and look for other sources of happiness. The same way training an animal gets reinforced when it finds food in a certain location, this reinforcement is the brain's way of telling us that we are on the right path. So when you are on the 'right' path, the path you chose, your brain will secrete endorphins to allow you to enjoy life's small wins, life's simple pleasures. You will end up reprogramming your brain through structure by allowing yourself to experience life, allowing yourself to realize your true potential for creation.

Temptation is minimal when you are following a structure. You leave less room for internal debate on what you have to do. If you set out and make a plan, FOLLOW IT. Don't you let your hot-headed cravings talk you out of the plan you set up with a cool-headed mind. Being inconsistent with yourself is dangerous and it will make you feel like you can't trust yourself, like you have no control. When you surrender control, you give up, and that's the real danger in addiction.

In the very early chapters we talked about how we are programmed and how we are conditioned to carry out a lot of behaviors, thoughts and even cravings automatically. Awareness and cognitive flexibility were the tools prescribed to release you from automatic behavior patterns. What will you do with this freedom? What will you do once you are aware? Will you put the next days, weeks, and months of your life into doing what matters to you? What fills you with vitality?

7

GREED, ENVY, AND CONSUMERISM

I n an epoch of comfort where you only need to push a button in order to get your food or clothing delivered to the doorstep of your home, you would think that people would be happy. Instead, suicide, depression, different types of addiction, and anxiety are all at an all-time high (Planap & Hest, 2019; SAMHSA, 2013; Stossel, 2013).

This is mainly due to the way materialism and consumerism affect us. They affect the hierarchy of our values, and lead us away from what is truly important to us. They provide us with temporary pleasures that don't do a very good job at satisfying our intrinsic needs.

Consumerism turns into a coping strategy, and this is how it becomes so deeply programmed into us. Let's use the satisfaction of hunger to better understand this concept. When you're hungry you can eat a high fiber meal such as lentils or you can have a piece of cheesecake. Both will meet your immediate need for hunger, but if you continue to use cheesecake to satisfy your need, over time, the high amount of sugar will have catastrophic effects on your body.

There are more beneficial coping strategies when you have a need that must be met. Talking to somebody, exercising, creating art are great examples of beneficial coping strategies. The less healthy coping strategies will work, but they do have long-term consequences.

I want you to realize why alcohol use disorders and addictions to pleasure are so prominent.

You are really not alone in this.

There's a reason why suicide, depression, anxiety, and addiction are all on the rise in our current era. It has to do with the Industrial Revolution, and later, the Technological Revolution. Our economic systems based on consumerism and the rise of social media bringing about instant social validation both cultivate the prioritization of junk values.

By junk values I mean values that are hollow and self-ish. Professor Tim Kasser (2002) has been researching the relationship between depression and hollow values for 25 years now. He has found a correlation between depression/anxiety and having what is called extrinsic values connected to obtaining more money and posses-sions, as well as wanting to be viewed highly by others. People who prioritize these materialistic values are more likely to succumb to depression and anxiety.

Intrinsic values are all the values we have been talking about up until this point. They are values related to making a difference, creating a positive change in the world, experiencing the world, and even our attitude towards suffering. The reward that is derived from these values comes from within. Extrinsic values are tied to external rewards, in these values you obtain your sense of self-worth from other people and through possessions.

One of the main problems with obtaining your sense of self-worth through your possessions is the way consumerism devalues your current possessions. There will always be an upgrade, and you will even be led to believe that you are inferior if you still have the older model of the new phone that came out. Using envy to motivate you to continue consuming, you will never experience true lasting satisfaction, since the very economic system is based on constant consumer dissatisfaction. If people were more or less satisfied, the general demand in the market would dwindle.

We have briefly talked about how your sense of self-worth should be grounded internally. When you base your self-worth on what other people think, it can make your self-esteem become very fragile, and ever-changing.

Extrinsic values include wanting to be physically attractive, having the latest car, the biggest home in order to attract attention. In other words, these materialistic values are tied to money, status, and admiration.

We all have a combination of both intrinsic and extrinsic values. The issue exists when we begin to sacrifice all our intrinsic values for materialistic ones. An example of this is working an excessive amount of overtime looking for a raise to improve your social status which sacrifices the intrinsic values of love and spending time with your family and loved ones.

A balance is required between these two types of values. Spending more of your time on intrinsic values will keep you happier, more fulfilled longer, consequently making it so you don't need to drink. Really think about how much time and energy you are putting into the things that matter most to you.

Our economic system reinforces hollow values, greed, envy, and instant gratification.

This race to consume, this competitive economic system we find ourselves in has deprived us of a sense of belonging, of a sense of community and cooperation. Individualism has risen and with it envy, nihilism (sense of meaninglessness) and hedonism (pursuit of pleasure and avoidance of pain).

There is a difference between envy and admiration of others. The difference between these two is similar to the difference between guilt and shame. Envy is based on a premise that you are not as good or that you feel inferior to others for your not having what they have. It's an attack to your self-worth, which can lead you to feel worthless. It's ok to learn from others, to look at others' success and recognize you have the capacity to thrive just like they have, but also be grateful for what you have. Being grateful for what you already have will lead to a general sense of satisfaction, and the side-effect will be progress.

Our economic system does not thrive on gratitude. It looks to devalue what you have so that you dispose of it and consume again. Consumerism teaches us that we should not be satisfied at any point. There is always an upgrade to your current cell phone, to your symbol of social status. This urge to purchase new items and be dissatisfied with old ones creates feelings of shame and envy within us. There is no room for gratitude in the way we are shown to live our lives. If you have an older phone, you may feel the need to belittle yourself before pulling out your phone by saying things like, "Yeah, I am going to pull out my dinosaur now."

The mechanism by which capitalism makes you want to consume more is through envy and shame. When you see somebody else with a new phone, it makes you want to catch up, it makes you want to acquire the new device.

We are taught that we should feel ashamed for not having the best car, or the biggest house. Consumerism tells us that these should be the things we strive for in life, these should be what we consider of value. Unfortunately, not everybody can live up to the standards that society imposes upon us. Unreal beauty standards, unnecessary purchasing of new products each year that do little but satiate a need to feel superior to others in turn disconnects us further from our community by making us individualistic and competitive.

The new items and the constant search for satisfaction replaces satisfaction itself as a social value transmitted to us by the media and more invasive forms of communication.

Consumerism portrays the constant attaining of materialistic goals as the only path to prosperity and happiness.

The underlying message ends up being, "Buy more stuff. Go to work. Feel better, so you can buy more stuff." For many people, consuming becomes one of their purposes in life (Campbell, 1989). If it truly made people happy, we might not be talking about it right now, but it really isn't fulfilling. People think that when they get that new house, they will be happy; when they finish their career, they will be fulfilled, and so on. They always have an excuse before they can be happy, a set of conditions that must be met first. If you follow this train of thought, you will never be satisfied. That is why gratitude is so important. You must be happy now, grateful for what you have now. You can progress, but be satisfied with what you have.

This is the problematic message that is being tossed around. People and objects are only good until the next best thing comes along, at which point you can dispose of the old. Do you think this applies to the way we treat each other as well?

Being placed at odds with others by the competitive nature of consumerism, we begin to feel that we are missing this sense of connection we long for, and this reinforces the fact that we are only obtaining approval through what we own. This gives us a fake sense of belonging, turning others into means by which we obtain pleasure, turning our relationships into things we can consume and dispose of once things get complicated or difficult. Have you ever met somebody who can't seem to stay in a relationship for more than a few months? They always seem to find something they don't like about the person. That's because there will always be something we don't like about everybody, nobody is perfect. Love is to choose to be with somebody in spite of the bad by remembering the good at all times. It's important to accept them and ourselves with our flaws.

Greed is another similarity consumerism shares with addiction.

The term 'binge' talks about a greedy way of life where we pursue pleasure and satisfaction no matter the cost, not thinking about the consequences. This type of attitude can tell us a thing or two about why our planet is in the state it's in. We look to produce and consume ever more since our economic system is based on continuous growth, never being satisfied. Our planet has limited resources, so this type of greedy search for development and consumption will have its consequences, but instant gratification blinds us of this fact.

It's interesting to see the similarities addiction shares with our systems of ecological exploitation. The addicted individual pursues pleasure and satisfaction without thinking too much about the consequences, caring only about instant gratification. If we only care about instant gratification, we are not thinking about the future consequences, or the impact our actions may have on others. Instant gratification is selfish and individualistic by nature.

In order to properly introduce the link between addictions and consumerism let's define the term of *binging*. The concept of binge is characterized by the excessive, impulsive, and uncontrolled consumption of an object in a limited period of time, by a feeling of loss of control, by an excessive sensibility for boredom and the search for ever-new sensations, and finally by distorted self-esteem (Passini, 2013, p.371)

The characteristics of an individual with a tendency to binge are those of a person who has trouble being aware of a sense of temporality. They aren't likely to think beyond the present moment. Also, there is a preference for action over thought, along with the inability to provide themselves feedback. By providing ourselves feedback, I am referring to the construct we call 'conscience.' Your conscience can make you pause and think twice before doing something. Since people with binging tendencies such as addictive personality types prefer action over thought by being impulsive, there is very little room for your conscience to speak to you.

The structure we call conscience is a term that was well studied and defined by the father of psychoanalysis, Sigmund Freud. He called it the Superego. According to psychoanalysis, our conscience is built through the internalization of social norms imposed first by our parents and later on by the state, school, or religion. We begin to draw our moral compass from our interactions with these social institutions (Freud, 1973).

What kinds of values and social norms are being transmitted by our consumerist cultures?

Institutions like school, state, and church have lost their influential powers to direct. Our relationship to authority has changed. People now look for their own senses of direction through other sources such as social media.

We can't allow the media to tell us what's important in life, we have to be able to look inside ourselves and choose our own paths. A lot of us begin drinking because it's a socially acceptable activity. It isn't only socially acceptable, it's actually considered 'cool.' The message that is transmitted to us is that life is only about fun, that we should always be happy, and that if you're not happy you're doing something wrong. If you had a rough day don't sit there and sulk about it, have a drink!

Tolerance being another factor of a greedy way of life is a scary thought. Our greed makes us want more and our tolerance makes us need more. How can this way of life affect our planet? Is it sustainable? As our tolerance builds up, so does our constant dissatisfaction leading to an ever increasing desire for more. This is great for consumerism to thrive. Unfortunately, greed is not only looked at as normal in our society, it's actually necessary for our current economic system to continue to sustain itself.

When we live without concern for anybody but ourselves, we start to harm others. There is a great economic inequality in the times we live and there isn't going to be anything left for the generations to come, either.

That's the truth of the matter, as Passini (2013) states, the pursuit of pleasure is an individualistic selfish pursuit. We look to feel pleasure at the expense of those around us, and we don't even end up happy. Transcending yourself and being of service to others will bring you much longer lasting fulfillment, than blindly chasing after different forms of instant gratification such as drinking.

Like I said consumerism is based on dissatisfaction. A product that would satisfy you in a long lasting manner isn't profitable and, as you may know, alcohol is quite profitable. The market needs to play on our needs; satisfying those needs indefinitely is just not good for business. That's particularly why the products we consume must be designed in a disposable fashion, forcing us to consume again by creating more dissatisfaction.

Consumerism "associates happiness not so much with the gratification of needs [...], as with an ever rising volume and intensity of desires, which imply in turn prompt use and speedy replacement of the objects intended and hoped to gratify them" (Bauman, 2007, p. 31 as cited in Passini, 2013).

Consumer culture prefers impulsivity over reflection. You need people to spend their money without thinking too much about the consequences or about the debt they might get themselves in. What matters is the way consuming is going to make us feel right this second. Patience and postponing pleasure become nearly impossible due to the way we are being programmed.

If you're not able to postpone gratification, then you wouldn't be able to choose to go for a run over having a drink. You wouldn't be able to choose to do any sort of work over more pleasurable activities. So instant gratification becomes an extremely dangerous habit for people who suffer from alcohol use disorders. This inability to delay gratification and the lack of self-reflection that society stimulates in us leave no doubt to how society can be creating more addictive personalities.

A lack of self-reflection is reinforced and required by consumerism. We need people to spend their money in the spur of the moment without thinking about consequences. People must be trained in only caring about how they feel right now. Impulsivity and extrinsic values are cultivated by consumerism.

Acting impulsively and only thinking about your short-term satisfaction prevents people from feeling responsible for their actions. Their loss of control is just shrugged off by saying, "I just do what I feel like doing," not realizing that they're not really in control of themselves. Living in a non-reflected automatic fashion makes it easy for consumerism to control you. They will just play on your likes and dislikes, pulling and repelling you as they wish, since there is no space to reflect upon your actions.

This is why people end up blaming 'the system,' but blaming the system is just following the trend of not taking accountability for your own actions even further.

I'm not saying that everybody falls victim to consumerism. There are people who can live satisfying lives. This is due mainly to the fact that they can delay their gratification and even lean into discomfort. They do this because they have a greater goal or values that they always have on their mind.

Underneath impulsivity lies fear. There's a negative outlook towards the world, a certain sense of insecurity. Impulsive people are not sure if they are going to ever receive gratification, they're not confident that they'll reach their goals. Consuming now, pursuing instant gratification becomes far more attractive since it guarantees the individual that they will receive gratification without a doubt. Even if the instant gratification is of much less value, it will still be preferred over the goal that seems so distant that it may never even arrive.

We can see how consumerism can numb us into a constant state of comfort, the same way that drinking does. Slowly, but surely separating us from what really matters to us.

A cooperative world view as opposed to a competitive one can help satisfy the needs for connection and approval that you have much more than social status or physical attractiveness. The idea is to stop seeing people as obstacles, rivals, or objects that we use to further our goals. A utilitarian worldview will only lead you to feel even more disconnected.

What is termed valuable by our policies turns into what the media talks about, and this in turn makes it what matters to us. Our society is one of the ways in which we are told what our values should be.

How is progress measured in your society?

Most society's growth and prosperity are measured by the GNP/GDP of the state. So the way societies measure progress is through income, through money which in turn teaches us that obtaining money should be one of our core values.

The problem is that the more you focus on extrinsic values such as money, image, and status, the less valuable we will perceive values like egalitarianism, connection, personal growth, and altruism. Focusing on materialistic values will push out the more meaningful values, and the more focused you are on extrinsic values the more like you are to suffer from addictions and depression (Kasser, 2018).

When I had you search for your values in the previous chapter, how many of them were related to materialistic concerns? Wellbeing is associated with having more intrinsic values, so try to keep that in mind as you clarify and discover your values.

The more insecure you are the more you will gravitate towards materialistic values which will only bring less happiness consequently making you less secure (Kasser, 2018). Less fulfillment creates the existential void we have spoken about. Insecurity is arrived at through inconsistent family and social environments. It comes from neglectful or abusive parenting.

We look to fill that emptiness we feel from the hollow values we have been taught to pursue by drinking. This is why I want to ask you not to beat yourself up over your addiction. Take responsibility now that you are aware and create your change.

8

COURAGEOUS COMMITMENT, FORGIVENESS, AND RESILIENCE

The path to recovery isn't necessarily an adventure. A lot of it is adjusting to a routine and a structure that brings you, step by step, closer to your goals. Sometimes, you'll take one step forward towards your potential, sometimes a few steps back.

Up until this point, I have asked you to accept yourself, forgive yourself, and become aware of yourself. I asked for acceptance without judgment and awareness so that you liberate yourself from the conditioning of biology and consumerism.

Flexibility is the key to freedom and it is also the key to resilience.

There's an old Indian story about how the Ganges River would rip all the big pine trees from their roots but would leave the tall grass and Weeping Willows.

You see, resilience is not about being rigidly strong and unmovable, nor is it about having the unwavering willpower of an ox. It's about being flexible: if you don't bend, you break. Being flexible and adapting to each situation and each hardship and bouncing right back up is what is meant by this story. It's a story about resilience.

You can't control most things that occur in life, so you must adapt. If you relapse, forgive yourself, and bounce right back up. The key to resilience and being able to forgive yourself is to remember that you are not your mistakes. We all make mistakes, learn from them, use life's struggles to make us stronger just like a seed reaches for light through all the darkness in the soil.

After that, I asked you to be present in the moment, but we also talked about how only living in the present is what makes us impulsive and selfish. We need a balance between being present and keeping the consequences of our actions in mind. It's great to live life fluidly along with recognizing that time for reflection is very necessary, too. That's why planning is so important, so you can take the time to reflect about what consequences your actions will have. After you make the plan, you can flow, you can go through the process of creating and experiencing life in the present moment.

The structure you create and the plans that you make must be aligned with your values. You must set short achievable goals so that you don't get frustrated and to do that your goals must be clear. More of your goals should be based around intrinsic values which will satisfy your needs in a long lasting manner.

I gave you some tips on practical activities and food choices that can help you reach your goals. The food I recommend helps you detox your body and releases you from the addictive chemicals our consumerist societies have engineered to keep you consuming more. It isn't a coincidence that so many of most of the junk foods sold have extremely high levels of refined sugars.

Your planning should begin by making a shopping list of and making sure you follow that list. Purchase items that align with the structure I have provided: items with less than 25 grams of sugar, and at least 30 grams worth of fiber per day. Basically, stay away from overly processed foods such as soda, candy, tortilla, and potato chips.

Physical activity in your routine is particularly important because it can help you handle some of the symptoms caused by alcohol and sugar dependencies.

Remember, alcohol is a sugar after all. Schedule in 20 to 40 minutes of cardiovascular activity. If you have some sort of injury, swimming can be a good alternative.

Planning a structure helps your brain reduce the options of the things that you could do and it can help you stop acting on impulse. As you detox, you will gain freedom as well. You'll see that the battle against yourself will become easier with time. Now that you have a plan, you should be starting to realize what it is that you actually value in life.

Values should not be things you're trying to achieve or get. Values should be the ways you want to behave, how you treat others and yourself, the actions you take, and the way you interpret each experience in your life. As you move towards your values, who you want to be and where you want to go will become clearer to you. Discipline brings true freedom to choose, as opposed to obeying every impulse and craving that comes to you.

Relapse Prevention: Honor in Suffering

Relapse is such a common occurrence in the recovery process. That's why I want you to come to terms with the fact that you are likely to fail, and that you are likely to relapse. Accept that fact. Recovery isn't easy. Things will get worse before they get better. If you accept that fact, it will allow you to prepare better for when it does happen.

Now, knowing that you probably will relapse, do you still want to continue with your recovery process?

It takes courage to commit to recovery, knowing that you are likely to fail, knowing that things won't be perfect, but what are you going to do when you do fail?

Find the courage to relapse and to forgive yourself, commit and promise that you won't run away from yourself anymore, that you will be open to yourself, you will love yourself. Once you do this, you will have the freedom to choose to walk towards your purpose.

After the whole plan we have come up with, it's time to commit, it's time to take your life and empower yourself to create the change you desire all while being flexible in life's struggles.

Answer these questions out loud, please.

Are you ready to commit to a life of your own choosing?

Yes, I'm ready to design my life as I see fit.

Are you ready to be free from the shackles of addiction?

Yes, I am ready to take responsibility for my own actions, to stop being a slave to my impulses.

Are you ready to stop being a slave to consumerism?

Yes, I am ready to decide what's really important to me.

Are you ready to act in accordance to your path?

Yes, I am ready to take action towards my goals.

When you fail, because you may, will you get back up?

Yes, I will use every struggle to learn and become a better version of myself.

Forget about perfection and embrace your flaws. Take your addiction and turn it into a personal triumph! There's honor in the suffering you're going through. You're taking a first step to loving yourself, to accepting yourself. After you allow yourself to be loved with your flaws, so too will you be able to tolerate and love others despite their shortcomings.

Your values will remain as potentialities unless your actions make them a reality. Through committing to your values, and planning out steps towards your goals is how you will manifest the change you desire in your life.

When you set a goal use the following structure:

- Describe your specific goal. Be concrete. Avoid being vague.
- Describe the values underlying your goal.
- Describe the actions that you're going to take towards achieving your goal.
- Separated into smaller steps or smaller goals.
- Write down the time and date when you're going to take your first step.

Setting goals is more about discipline, and about being able to delay instant gratification. Your goals and your values will lead you straight into discomfort, so we must have the discipline to do the things we don't like, especially when we don't want to do them. We should only take the steps if they truly align with our goals in the long-term, of course.

Discipline is directly tied to patience. Why do you think it takes so long to get a university degree or a black belt in martial arts? The process itself is part of the reward because through the process you gain patience and discipline. The degree and the black belt are only symbols of the virtues you gain through the process. Discipline sounds like a chore to many of us, but it's in fact what liberates us from our habits.

Patience will derive from discipline, but in order to be patient, you need to be confident. You need to be sure that you're capable. It's a cycle, as you begin to achieve your goals, you will trust yourself more, and believe in yourself which will allow you to be more patient afterwards, since you know you will be able to reach your next goal.

If we fill our lives with activities that don't align with our goals you will soon have issues. You will feel bored, and boredom is one of the main reasons people relapse. Boredom arises when we feel that all our efforts are useless, or that we are stuck doing something irrelevant to our lives, something that doesn't bring us close to the things we value.

Some people are fine working at any kind of job because they know the money they make there will bring them closer to the things they value after work is over. There are other people however, that do have a need to feel like their skills are being put to good use. Some people need to do meaningful work. They need to be challenged everyday at work and can't stand monotony, and well those are linked to values in that person's life. Those decisions are very personal, that's why I said there is no right or wrong answer when it comes to values. There is, however, a correlation between more intrinsic values and higher levels of well-being, which translates into lower levels of addiction.

It's great if you're able to do work that isn't intrinsically valuable to you because it will bring you closer to other meaningful activities without getting bored or frustrated! Boredom and frustration will arise from not seeing value in the activities you do day to day, or because the activities you do day to day actually don't have any significance to what it is you're striving for.

Let's make a differentiation between goals and values. A goal is a step that will get you closer to being in alignment with your values. There will be gaps between the time you spend pursuing one goal and the next. In those gaps you may experience boredom or frustration, depending on what your attitude is towards the gaps.

If you're not able to work towards a particular goal, take your time to rest and relax, enjoy the process. If you can't create, then resort to your experiential values. Go out and live a little. Visit some friends, watch a movie, read a book. All these experiential activities will revitalize you, enabling you to work harder at your goals once the time comes again.

Finding meaning in your monotonous day to day tasks can be difficult, we can forget why it is that we do the things we do. This can lead to unmotivation, which is precisely what we are going to talk about next.

9

SELF-ACTUALIZATION AND MOTIVATION: A PATH TO FULFILLMENT

Hierarchy of Needs and Motives

To understand our motives to move and take action, let's refer back to the hierarchy of needs proposed by Abraham Maslow (1970). Maslow was a theoretical, clinical, and experimental psychologist who has greatly influenced the way we look at motivation. To this day, his findings are being applied in all sorts of settings including organizational settings. Companies apply these findings in order to keep their employees satisfied and motivated.

Maslow focused on the more positive aspects of human beings since he felt the pathological aspects received too much attention. He focused on human potential, and how to turn that potential into reality.

This hierarchy talks about our fundamental need to expand and find more ways to intercommunicate with our environment and the people in it. We have a tendency to want to connect to life through expression and experience. In order for us to be concerned with our most transcendental motivations, we first have to meet our most basic needs, otherwise survival will dominate our motivations and we will end up feeling like we aren't realizing our potential.

We talked about how we should use this hierarchy as a guide when prioritizing our values since that's how humans inherently function.

Physiological and Safety Needs and Motivations

The first set of needs are related to physiological needs. You need to have shelter from the heat and cold. you must be fed. You need physical activity. You must sleep. These needs are a priority and your body will let you know when these aren't being met satisfactorily.

Since these are the most important needs for us to progress and be able to focus on more complex motivations, these are the first aspects you're going to focus on when planning out your week. Each day, fit in at least 25 minutes of cardiovascular activity, get eight hours of quality sleep, reduce sugar intake, and increase dietary fiber consumption. This will be the best way to satisfy these needs so that you can look to the next step.

If our physiological needs aren't met, our motivations will revolve around them. If you look at Africa, you will hear about how a person may walk for four hours to obtain water for her family. This person's motivation lies solely on the first step of the pyramid without allowing much thought to anything else.

Our motivation is determined by unsatisfied needs. In general, most of us aren't functioning at the bottom level of the pyramid, so it doesn't motivate our behavior on a daily basis.

The next step on the pyramid is a need for safety or security that must be satisfied for us to progress towards realizing our potential. You need a structure and a predictable environment to feel safe. Job security and a place to call home are essential for you to stop thinking exclusively about your survival. You require this sense of security to stop living a life motivated by fear.

This need is evidenced in children. If an infant doesn't have a secure base, they won't be willing to explore their environment or even play with toys. The secure base for children is normally the primary caregiver (Bretherton, 1992).

The feeling of safety is internalized by all of us as long as we had a predictable and stable environment. Consistency and structure in our lives generate that positive outlook towards the life we have been talking about. It allows us to feel free to explore and experience all that life has to offer us.

At any time within this process of meeting our needs and looking for higher motives, we can make the decision of stepping back into safety or moving forward into growth. If you have not been able to resolve the lower levels of needs, your motivations are going to be stuck focused there. Just like it could be difficult to appreciate a sunset, or look at beautiful flowers while you're on an empty stomach, or while you fear for your safety.

The first two steps on the pyramid are largely preoccupied with survival. Our motivation is just to make a living, just to make it by, so when we are stuck in this phase of life, it becomes really difficult to think about others. Thinking about justice becomes a distant idea when you are struggling to put food on the table. Many of us get stuck on these first two steps, leaving the rest of the needs in the pyramid unsatisfied, making us generally unsatisfied with our current lifestyle.

What's most unfortunate is that when we're trapped in the lower levels, the higher needs on the pyramid seem unimportant. We view them as unreal, or unnecessary.

When I mention that having more extrinsic needs is correlated with less well-being, I don't mean to say that people can live without caring about financial security. Financial security is the way we feel safe in our environment, having a secure base allows us to explore other interests and cultivate our passions. Attaining excessive wealth does not correlate with more happiness (Kasser, 2002). Once you meet your financial needs to the point that you don't have to worry about paying rent on time, you can start focussing on higher needs and less selfish values.

Job security and motivation are often influenced by needs of recognition, appreciation, and safety. If you value mastery and challenge, it means that you might not do well in a monotonous 9-to-5 job, it means you have a need to be intellectually stimulated so that you can express your potential. Not everybody values that need as much. Some people don't want to take chances on a job that might not work out and prefer a slow, steady, and safe route to their goals. A stable and predictable job can be more relaxing for a person who values safety and stability. There's more than one path to arrive at the same destination. You have to evaluate your priorities.

Belonging and Esteem, Needs and Motivations

The next two steps of the pyramid revolve around esteem and belonging. These needs are social in nature and are no longer focused on survival. They're more focused on status, accomplishment, relationships, and loving yourself.

It's difficult to conceive that anybody would feel disconnected in the age of the internet. People used to write a letter and wait weeks or even months for a distant friend or relative to receive it, and now, when we can chat instantly with friends who live around the world, loneliness is at an all-time high in our current societies (Guo, 2018).

Online interactions have replaced a lot of the face-to-face exchanges people would have had. You would think that interaction would be satisfying whether it is virtual or not. Loneliness and the rise of the internet tell us otherwise, since people don't seem to be having their need for belonging met (Guo, 2018).

Loneliness is based on perception. You can have a lot of social interactions and still feel lonely. You can be socially isolated, or have few interactions, and feel perfectly fine. In other words, loneliness means that you are lacking a specific type of interaction in your life. Perhaps it's a supportive, stimulating, or challenging relationship that you're missing.

The problem with the types of virtual interactions that we have links back to a consumerist tendency of social media.

Social media promotes extrinsic values where you gain your worth through others' validation. A large part of interactions that people have on social media have a need for validation at heart. These interactions satisfy our needs much like a cheesecake that satisfies our hunger. Likes on social media give you a sense of acceptance and satisfy your needs for interaction without really giving you a long-lasting sense of belonging because the characteristics you're being rewarded for are mostly superficial in nature.

Interacting online is easier because you don't really need to deal with the elements of face-to-face interactions that cause people social anxiety. This fact makes it so people lose the social skills required to engage in meaningful ways which further the feelings of alienation experienced. "Lonely people are dissatisfied with their offline relations due to deficient social skills; they turn to using more of online communications for compensation" (Kim, LaRose, & Peng, 2009, p.452 as cited in Guo, 2018).

When we're addicted to a substance or behavior, we often become impulsive. Impulsivity makes it so we don't think things through. If we don't think, it's difficult for us to be aware of the consequences our actions might have on others. This is why narcissism is often associated with addiction, it's because of its impulsive nature. The selfish tendencies described previously aren't necessarily intentional. A lot of the time selfishness is just a side-effect of living a pleasure centered life, an impulsive lifestyle.

Addiction and social media have their correlations. People who have more narcissistic, self-centered, or selfish tendencies will be more prone to overindulging in the pleasures provided by the attention received through social media (Guo, 2018). Pleasure derived from obtaining admiration from others. As we've discussed previously, this is because we base our sense of self-worth externally.

This need for admiration which leads us to portray an ideal version of ourselves on social media can create lower levels of self-esteem in others as well. People who look to social media to get an idea of what reality is like, only see other people's ideal selves which makes them think everybody is better than them. These perceptions distort what should be important to us and teaches us to draw our sense of self-worth externally.

Narcissism is an individualistic way of life based mostly on extrinsic values. This is what we're trying to avoid in our work. When you're not able to see your own flaws, you start blaming others for your shortcomings, you begin to project your flaws onto those around you. If you're perfect, and something goes wrong, it couldn't have possibly been your fault, so you look to blame the first target that comes by. Living with a narcissist is terribly difficult because they often consider them-selves to be right.

This is another black and white way of looking at life. Narcissists are all good, therefore everybody else is all bad; they don't trust anybody else's judgment but their own. Through their attitude and unrealistic demands, narcissists become increasingly lonely and disconnected.

Pulling away from a selfish lifestyle where we seek comfort at all costs is exactly what is required to change the relationship you have with drinking. It's important to think about the consequences, about how these consequences may affect others, and how they can impact your own future. Not wanting to be perfect and accepting your own flaws will help you battle those feelings of shame that stimulate your self-deprecating tendencies.

Social media is a great medium of communication for narcissists. Narcissism can be looked at as not accepting yourself, not accepting your flaws. Not embracing your shadow leads to narcissism, and social media allows these people to portray their ideal selves as a reality. They can control which parts of their life people can and can't see. Social media is instrumental in fueling their need to be admired by others instantly much like the rush you get from a drug.

We may associate socializing with partying and some of us especially associate it with drinking. As I have stated previously, there are other ways to meet people.

The way the needs in this category are fulfilled is by cultivating your talents, finding what it is you love doing and doing it well. Then you will find like-minded people who inspire and appreciate your progress. This will make you feel like you're contributing to society. Not mastering anything in life will make you feel like you're good at nothing, it'll make you feel worthless. Spending a certain amount of energy on mastery is one of the motivating drives in our lives.

Not following your motives leaves you without motivation. This should be intuitive but we don't even know why we do the things we do. This hierarchy of needs is meant to help you if at any point you feel lost. It's one of the ways we can connect with our internal sense of direction.

Success is found when you find a balance between being safe and feeling appreciated. You may find that balance when you find work that is meaningful to you.

When you're not passionate about what you create, about what you contribute to the world, it will make it so your need for esteem won't be met, since you will be perceived as not contributing anything of value. Without passion, going the extra mile or excelling professionally is rather impossible. Mediocrity is so common due to high levels of conformity, sticking to values that were imposed to you, and not cultivating your own gifts and talents.

Self-Actualizing Needs and Motives

This need is of the highest nature. It's our need for purpose, to find meaning in life. When your current self doesn't match your ideal self, it means this need isn't satisfied. This, of course, will always be the case since there will always be potential for growth.

The last step of the pyramid is about leaving your legacy, about giving back to the community by creating change in the world. Many of us don't ever get to that point, which is why regret and depression are so prominent in our era.

According to our review of the pyramid of needs, all of our behaviors are motivated by needs. The last step on the pyramid is a transcendental step, it's realizing our potential. It's still a need, though. Just as if we were not to eat, not meeting this need will have detrimental effects on us. Not meeting your self-actualizing need will leave you with a feeling of stagnation and meaninglessness.

"Musicians must make music, artists must create, poets must write if they are to be ultimately at peace with themselves. What human beings can be, they must be. They must be true to their own nature. This need we may call self-actualization... It refers to man's desire for self-fulfillment, namely to the tendency for him to become actually in what he is potentially" (Maslow, 1943, p. 203.).

Fulfilling your need to create goes well beyond survival or approval. Self-actualization doesn't have to be artistic in nature, though. Art is a very common means by which people fulfill their need for purpose since art is an act of creating and expressing what's on the inside in ever more complex ways. Your fulfillment can be reached in the joy you receive by taking care of your family and making sure your children have a fair chance at choosing what their purpose is.

Fulfilling this need will chase away any need to escape, those feelings of boredom, and any emptiness we have. The existential void a lot of us carry is evidence of just how important it is for us to realize our potential.

Self-actualizing people become detached from the need of social approval and social comparison. They don't strive to be better than anybody else, and instead only compare themselves to their previous selves.

Peak Experiences and Creativity

There are still plenty of mysteries to be solved when it comes to who we are and how consciousness is possible. There are experiences that place us in touch with these aspects of life and make us question our reality. It's yet another exciting part of life that is worth exploring. There's much more to reality than we actually know.

One final comment about people who satisfy their need for self-actualization is necessary. During his time as a psychotherapist, Maslow focused on working and interviewing extremely successful individuals. Most other psychologists of his time focused on working on helping people overcome their illnesses. Maslow looked instead to focus on people's positive aspects to help them realize their potential.

Maslow was interested in understanding what made these successful individuals function, how they got to be so happy and wealthy. During his time studying these people, he noticed a common trend. A large majority of these successful people he spoke to describe having what Maslow called a 'Peak Experience.' In fact, most of these individuals reported having several of those experiences in their lifetime. These experiences were thought to be a symptom of having satisfied their self-actualization need.

A peak experience is popularly known as a mystical experience. These occurrences have been reported since ancient times. Joan of Arc reported having these experiences all throughout her life, for example. Nikola Tesla and Steve Jobs are more recent examples of people who accredited a large amount of their creativity to these experiences.

Peak experiences seem to be able to naturally occur in our brains, without the need of any exterior chemicals. For some reason, they occur more often in self-actualizing individuals. Some people look to induce these states through years of breathwork much like monks at the monasteries. Transpersonal psychology has grown to value these experiences and even go as far as to say that they are imperative for a person's well-being.

These experiences are characterized by feelings of one-with-allness, a certain dissolution of the self where the limits of self and everything else seem to be removed. During these states of mind, people report feeling interconnected with other people and nature.

This type of feeling could most definitely reinforce the idea of cooperation versus competition that we have been speaking of. Feeling like we are part of nature and internalizing this idea will help us feel less lonely, and we will look at the relationship between ourselves and those around us differently.

We would be less prone to hurt our loved ones since empathy comes with feelings of connectedness. Our empathy can extend towards the planet we live in and the way we need it as much as it needs us.

Internalizing this feeling of connectedness will allow you to satisfy your need for connection chasing away loneliness. You won't find yourself drinking out of loneliness as often if you're able to see your place in nature, society, and the universe.

The feeling of one-with-allness isn't the only benefit obtained from a mystical experience. The fact that boundaries are dissolved is of great importance, too. By boundaries, I mean that categories are dissolved.

To better understand this concept of dissolving categories we can look to dreams, which are extremely important, as we have mentioned. There are two types of memory that we mainly use when we dream: episodic memory and semantic memory.

Episodic memory is our memory of time and space-specific events. When we think of a time when we were at a friend's house, for example, this memory is tied to a place and a time. Semantic memory is the memory associated with concepts like a banana being part of the fruit category.

When we dream, cortisol disrupts these memory systems, particularly during the REM sleep stage (Payne & Nadel, 2004). What happens is that episodic memory is shut down. So when we dream we might dream of a person and a place that never coexisted at the same time or at the same place. Maybe you had a dream about being on a cruise ship with your boss, which probably never really happened. We start to mix distant unrelated memories and concepts together in ways they had never been mixed before.

Mystical experiences and dreams alike serve a critical function in our ability to be creative. When your brain tears down all the categories and limits that exist, it allows us to mix concepts and ideas in new and different ways, giving room to creation.

Alchemists have always said that destruction (dissolutions of our self and the tearing down of categories) and creation are two parts of the same process. In order to create, you must first make room by destroying. To create a new version of yourself, you have to tear down all the behavior patterns and coping mechanisms you have built.

This mixing of ideas is the way that new creations are born, new paths in our brain are created, and others are reinforced, helping us look at life in a different perspective. We can take life's pleasure for granted at times. By deconstructing our old habits, we can learn to create new associations. These are moments where light can seep in through the cracks. Take advantage of those difficult moments to gain a better understanding of what lies beneath you and to come to know what you truly think is important. If you're fed up with life and you reach a breaking point, it's probably because there's something in your life that you need to pay attention to, something that needs to change. Don't just brush it off as an emotional weakness or a tantrum.

Deconstructing yourself will help you realize that drinking isn't a personality trait, it isn't what makes you, you! Pay attention to your dreams, pay attention to your emotional breakdowns, and pay attention to your existential crises.

More and more research points to the possibility that one of the reasons we have taken such a large evolutionary leap from other primates is due to these experiences. This may explain why shamans have engaged in these sorts of mystical experiences since the beginning of civilization (Winkelman, 2017).

As you allow your sleep cycles to normalize and stop sedating yourself, your creativity will also come back, allowing you to approach life in a much more flexible and dynamic fashion.

Self-actualization is based on the actualizing principle of the universe. The universe is ever-expanding. It's growing and finding new ways to interconnect in ever more complex manners. This same tendency is theorized to exist within us as well. Perhaps you have heard the old axiom, :As above, so below." Or perhaps you've discovered the writings at the Temple of Apollo that say, "Know thyself, and thou shalt know the universe and God."

It's meant to be our underlying purpose, to grow ever more complex, and to connect in increasingly complex ways with the universe. Our purpose is to evolve, thrive, and reach our true potential.

Life's Beauty and Staying Motivated

What good is having clear values and a purpose if you don't have the motivation to make your imagined values become a reality in your life?

Setting a goal isn't enough to get you motivated. You have to actually connect with your goal for you to care. You have to be passionate about what you're doing. You must find a way to relate to your goals, and that means that your values have to match the goals that you set. Goals must take you closer to what you actually find important in your life for you to be determined and stay motivated.

Are you choosing your own goals?

Might there be something else that you feel more connected to?

To stay motivated on your path of recovery, you can set up a reward system, a means by which you can celebrate how well you have done. Allow yourself to have fun, but make sure the fun that you're having aligns with your values. Allow yourself to fill the gaps between your goals with experiences that are meaningful to you.

Choosing your path is extremely motivating. One of the main factors in losing motivation is the feeling of being stuck, the feeling of not having any independence. An example is when you are forced to carry out a job that you find irrelevant to your path. It's important for you to pay attention to this feeling of being stuck, it means you feel stagnant. You may not be including enough of your intrinsic values into your life and that will lead to frustration and emptiness.

Another way you can stay motivated is by making and maintaining meaningful relationships. Engage with people you share passions with, people that inspire you.

Social learning is critical to all animals. Unfortunately, our society doesn't reward the community as much as it does competition which is why you may feel weak when you look to others for advice or support.

Find people that challenge you and question you. Having friends you feel comfortable around is great too, since we do have a need for security, but finding people who challenge you helps you grow by placing you outside your comfort zone. People that provide constructive criticism do so because they see that you have the potential to change and learn.

Another way to revitalize yourself is by giving yourself permission to take a break. Plan a vacation, and do something different to allow yourself to press the reset button on your brain. When you come back from your activity, if it was refreshing and different enough to your daily routine, you can come back and see things in a new light allowing yourself to become motivated once more.

A monotonous routine can get to you, so it's important to seek new stimulus every so often. A routine is only monotonous if you perceive it to be so. Not everybody has the same needs and values. The important part is to do it in a planned manner while having your own permission. Remember, we're trying to stick to a structure.

The best way to do this is to go to events that interest you. When I say an event, it can be something like a fair that's passing through town, or an academic talk somebody is going to give, attend conferences related to topics that excite you, take workshops where you can learn new skills. If you are open-minded, you can find plenty of activities to participate in. This, of course, would be assuming that you live in a fairly populated city. Some of the best ways to become aware of events in your region is through social media; you would be surprised at just how much is going on at any given time.

If you live in a more rural setting, then I'm sure there are other types of activities that you can pursue such as fishing, swimming, hiking, hunting, and animal watching.

You can meet like-minded people of all sorts, and expose yourself to new ways of looking at the world and in your interests. This can rekindle your passions toward life. Cultivate your interests. If you feel any hint of an interest in a particular part of life like dancing, writing, drawing, fighting, anything at all, you should explore it.

We're not born with passions. We catch glimpses of interests along our way in life. If there is something that interests you, pursue it, even if it's just in an exploratory fashion. We have to work on our interests so we can turn them into passions. Only through dedication do you become passionate about anything in life.

This tendency to explore and to find new stimulation is often replaced by drinking. A lot of people look to 'get wild' by going out and partying. This is really just another way of noticing that you may be lacking adventure in your sober life. Try new things, meet new people, go to new places.

The idea is to keep yourself from falling into a feeling of stagnation. You don't have to stick to a single interest, or even learn something new every few months. Simply check to see how bored or uninterested you have become with life to tell you whether or not you are ready to pursue a new interest. As I said, even interests take discipline and dedication. Relationships and communicating with others is one of the best ways to be exposed to aspects of life that may interest you.

Can you describe the type of person you would like to meet?

Become that person yourself. Become the person you would like to have in your life.

Connecting with your values and cultivating your talents will help you enter a state of flow in life where you're simply living and enjoying life. Once you're in that state, people will notice. They will gravitate towards you because people notice when somebody enjoys the life they're living.

Once you start making meaningful connections with people, you will start realizing just how awesome it is to be alive. Finding people that appreciate and accept you for who you are is truly priceless. It's one of the most comforting and motivating sensations one can experience, like being there for them when they need you.

Finding what you're good at and doing it makes you feel so valuable. You won't want to continue drinking, you will feel like it's distracting you from doing the things you truly love. Drinking will fall out of favor with you once you cultivate your talent. There's so much more to live for. You have the potential to be truly great.

Once you begin to break free from limiting beliefs, you start being able to see all the actual options and opportunities you have in life. There are so many opportunities to grow, but also to simply enjoy life. A whole world begins to unfold for you.

I really don't know what more we could ask for when life and the world is growing in ever more complex ways, and we get the opportunity to be part of it all. We're in one of the most awesome times to be alive.

There are projects to set up colonies on Mars and the Moon. Soon we'll be able to talk to each other without even speaking a word using Elon Musk's Neuralink. Sometime in the future, it's going to be difficult to distinguish artificial intelligence systems from actual living beings. People are going to be able to genetically engineer their children very soon. So many of the biological predispositions to disease may become things of the past.

There's so much going on right now, it's just a matter of looking around and appreciating the whole picture.

Non-profit organizations like Search for Extraterrestrial Intelligence (SETI) are monitoring the skies daily. They've found large amounts of planets with Earth-like conditions where life could be possible. Wouldn't it be great to know that we're not alone, that there are other societies that have faced similar struggles, and surpassed them? Isn't that an inspiring thought? These and many more are some of the big changes and experiences we can hope for in the coming years.

Never before have our societies been so accepting of each persons' individuality and their rights. In these times you get to be who you want to be, you get to choose your path. In some ways, we've never been so free. All we need to do is pitch in and believe in ourselves. We only need to believe in ourselves until we actually see what we're capable of. After that, you will know just how much potential you have. Belief will no longer be required.

You're a part of life. You don't have to sit idly by and watch how everything unfolds. You can take action and help come up with solutions to life's struggles and mysteries.

Little by little, you will start to appreciate all the beauty life has to offer. You will become passionate about protecting it, about taking care of yourself, and loving all that is important to you.

CONCLUSION

In most of this work, I provided you more questions than answers. This is precisely because I don't have the answers: you do!

The questions I asked you are questions everybody should be asking themselves.

Society has given us the answers to our questions before we even knew the questions existed. This is simply not fair.

After waking up, you may have feelings of contempt towards society, and maybe even towards your parents for not allowing you to pick your own path. This is normal, but we need to forgive our parents and society since they have been hypnotized the same way we have been.

As for society, we can only change our surroundings by first changing ourselves, and hopefully influencing others around us.

Don't forget that you too were once deeply asleep. Don't forget that you, too, did not think about where you came from or about where you're going. Don't judge others who haven't had the opportunity to wake up. Don't claim superiority over them.

The fact that you may gain more insight and more freedom over yourself makes you more responsible, too. You're now responsible for helping others wake up, you're not responsible for judging them.

Compassion and empathy are the keys to showing others the path. Your message won't be heard if you criticize people from a place of false superiority.

At the beginning of this work I asked you to keep a question in mind.

Why did you want to recover?

The answer to that question is the only fuel you need to stay motivated.

Your fears and doubts can distract you from your path but only momentarily. You need to remember that you are not your fears. Listen to them, but remember your own value as you move through life.

"Keep your mind ever on the Star, but let your eyes watch over your footsteps, lest you fall into the mire by reason of your upward gaze" (Initiates, 2014, p. 40).

Be present and keep your mind connected to your values: this is where you will draw the strength to continue through the worst of times.

Recognize the mistakes you have made up until now and show that you want to change through your actions. You are NOT your mistakes. You ARE much more than that time you got drunk and cheated on your partner. You aren't inherently bad, you CAN change. That is what is so wonderful about imperfection.

You may have noticed that as our work progressed, we focused less and less on thinking about all the problems that drinking has brought, and looked instead to the aspects of life you should be focusing on.

In this same way, start to bring more meaningful activities that really do matter more to you. Naturally, drinking will fade away. It's importance will die out once you realize what truly matters to you.

I truly feel that we are all destined for far more than our economic systems have led us to believe. We have been blinded to our true potential. We have come to think that we're only as valuable as how much we are financially worth.

There is more than one path to the same destination. Only you can choose your path, nobody can ever choose it for you.

Thank you for reading my book Quit Drinking. If you have enjoyed reading it perhaps you would like to leave a star rating and a review for me on Amazon? It really helps support writers like myself create more books. You can leave a review for this book by scanning the QR code below:

Thank you so much. Rebecca Dolton

Made in United States
North Haven, CT
27 January 2022